Case studies in the neuropsychology of reading

edited by

Elaine Funnell
Royal Holloway University of London, UK

Psychology Press
a member of the Taylor & Francis group

Psychology Press Ltd, Publishers
27 Church Road
Hove
East Sussex BN3 2FA
UK

British Library Cataloguing-in-Publication Data
A catalogue record for this book is available from the British Library

ISBN: 0-86377-558-6 (hbk)

Typeset by Action Publishing Technology, Gloucester, UK
Printed and bound in the UK by
Biddles Ltd, Guildford and King's Lynn

Contents

Contributors

H. Branch Coslett, Center for Cognitive Neuroscience, Department of Neurology, Temple University School of Medicine, 3401 North Broad St., Philadelphia, PA19140, USA.

Andrew W. Ellis, Department of Psychology, University of York, York YO1 5DD, UK

Elaine Funnell, Psychology Department, Royal Holloway University of London, Egham, Surrey TW20 0EX, UK

Alison Hunter, Speech and Language Therapy Department, Monkgate Health Centre, York

Matthew A. Lambon Ralph, Department of Psychology, University of York, York YO1 5DD, UK; and MRC Cognition and Brain Sciences Unit, 15 Chaucer Road, Cambridge CB2 2EF, UK

Jackie Masterson, University of Essex, Wivenhoe Park, Colchester, Essex, CO4 3SQ, UK

Julie Morris, Department of Psychology, University of York, York YO1 5DD, UK; and Department of Speech, University of Newcastle, Newcastle-upon-Tyne, UK

Karalyn Patterson, MRC Cognition and Brain Sciences Unit, 15 Chaucer Road, Cambridge CB2 2EF, UK

Eleanor M. Saffran, Center for Cognitive Neuroscience, Department of Neurology, Temple University School of Medicine, 3401 North Broad St., Philadelphia, PA 19140, USA

Introduction

Elaine Funnell
Royal Holloway University of London, UK

Far from abating, after a century of research, the interest in the psychology of reading continues to grow. One might, perhaps, have expected that a learned skill, such as reading, which is superimposed on more basic cognitive mechanisms, would have yielded its secrets long ago. But new questions continue to be asked; new journals on reading continue to appear; undergraduates continue to hone their research skills by carrying out experiments on reading; and research projects on reading continue to attract funding.

One reason for this lively interest is that the understanding of reading processes is not after all a readily tractable problem. Another is that, as the search for understanding has continued, new theoretical questions, methodological issues, and technological advances have evolved to challenge current thinking. Now, the different approaches to reading behaviour—adult skilled reading, reading development, acquired and developmental dyslexia—traditionally considered to be independent issues, are intertwined. Computer simulations of reading processes are available to mimic normal reading performance based on particular theoretical positions; and subsequent damage to the system can be used to test theories of dyslexia. Functional brain imaging studies of normal and impaired reading can be used to examine brain correlates of normal and impaired reading.

As a result of this activity, theories of reading processes and reading development, and the methods used to investigate reading, have become more sophisticated. It is not a simple matter to step freshly into the area of reading and carry out research. The complexities of the reading stimuli employed and the theoretical implications of their use have to be appreciated; the nuances of the different theoretical positions have to be understood. This is not easy, particularly for those entering the world of reading from another discipline, since the work is spread over many articles, in many different sources, published over many years.

The purpose of this book is to provide an accessible, up-to-date review of work on the main forms of acquired dyslexia and one form of developmental dyslexia—developmental surface dyslexia. The review is presented through the discussion of case studies selected to represent important milestones in

1

the development of knowledge. Case studies range from old to new, and form the basis for a discussion of a particular type of disorder and its role in the development of theory, often spanning a time from before the point at which the case was reported, to well beyond. Unexplored aspects of the disorder are mentioned; blind alleys pointed out; implications for treatment are discussed; and questions raised for the future. Reports of computer simulations and brain imaging studies, where these are available, are included.

Sophisticated methods lie at the heart of the study of reading and reading disorders and need to be understood if the theoretical accounts of reading processes are to be fully appreciated. For this reason, this short introduction to the book will cover the main methodological issues in reading in preparation for later chapters. Those who need more background to the field are recommended to read the excellent introduction to reading, writing, and dyslexia by Ellis (1993).

STIMULI AS THE KEY TO READING PROCESSES

Reading research uses a powerful and elegant set of stimuli composed of various types of words and nonwords. In the English language particularly, with its complex relationship between the spelling and pronunciation of written words, the use of different types of words and nonwords provides the key to the processes involved in reading. Performance on different types of words can be measured and the results used to detect the influence of particular processes in normal and abnormal reading. Theories of reading are based upon these findings. Since the nature of the stimuli used in reading research is so fundamental to the enterprise, a brief introduction to the main types of stimuli might be useful here.

The English language contains many *irregular* words, such as *pint* and *yacht*. These words do not follow the most common pronunciation of the individual letters or letter groups in the word and so cannot be read aloud successfully using a purely phonic method. If a phonic method was used, then *pint* would be pronounced to rhyme with "mint" and *yacht* to rhyme with "matched". For successful reading aloud, particularly when words are presented out of context, written irregular words must be recognised as familiar written forms. When written irregular words are pronounced correctly, it signifies that the words are represented in the subject's reading vocabulary and, for this reason, irregular words are used as a test of word-based (or *lexical*) processes.

In contrast to irregular words, words with *regular* spelling-to-sound correspondences, such as *thing* and *shampoo*, can be read aloud correctly using knowledge of the most common pronunciation of particular letters and letter groups. This knowledge is considered to be *sub-lexical*, since it operates on graphemes, rather than on complete written word forms. Graphemes are letters and letter groups that represent single sounds (or *phonemes*). Normal readers typically use their sub-lexical knowledge to read unfamiliar written words. When they do so, they pronounce unfamiliar regular words more successfully than unfamiliar irregular words. This difference is referred to as the "regularity effect". If people fail to show a regularity effect when reading unfamiliar regular and irregular words, it suggests that sub-lexical knowledge is either not available to them, or has not been applied.

Not all languages lend themselves readily to the investigation of distinctions between lexical and sub-lexical oral reading processes. Italian and Spanish, for example, are composed almost entirely of regular words that can be pronounced phonically, so that, in principle, a Spanish or Italian reader could read text aloud without establishing a lexical system. In these languages it is difficult to find classes of words that can readily distinguish between the use of lexical and sub-lexical processes (but see Chapter 5 for novel methods for accessing dyslexia in regular languages). The study of the breakdown of reading alphabetic script in languages other than English, and in languages with non-alphabetic scripts such as Chinese and Japanese, has considerably broadened our understanding of the role of lexical and sub-lexical processes involved in oral reading. The study of acquired reading across languages is an important area of research that regrettably cannot be done justice to here.

Returning to the English language, regular words are not a pure test of sub-lexical processing because *familiar* written regular words are likely to be within the subject's reading vocabulary and so represented in the lexicon. For a pure test of sub-lexical processing, *nonwords*, such as *vib*, *chickor*, *spote*, are used. People who fail to show a regularity effect when reading words are unlikely to be able to read nonwords successfully.

Of course, written words need to be understood, as well as recognised, and one type of word—the *homophone*—is ideally suited to test this. When homophones, such as *pear*, *pair*, and *pare* are presented in isolation, there are no cues to the meaning of the word apart from the orthographic configuration. Yet, most of us would be able to assign meaning to each of these words. This shows that there must be a process that maps written words directly onto word meanings. However, sometimes people read aloud the homophone correctly, but then give the wrong meaning, supplying the meaning of a different homophone instead: saying, for example, that *pear* means "two of something". When this happens, it shows that the person has based the knowledge of word meaning on the sound of the word, and not on the printed form. This may occur even for irregular words, such as *bury*, which may be pronounced correctly but then defined as an alternative homophone: in this case as meaning "a small fruit" (i.e. berry). When this happens, it is taken as evidence that the written word has been recognised as a familiar written word form (and so processed lexically) and mapped directly onto its spoken lexical word form without prior access to word meaning.

From this brief introduction to these different types of stimuli—regular and irregular words, homophones, and nonwords—it is possible to demonstrate three reading procedures with rather different characteristics. The first procedure accesses the meaning of familiar written words, directly from print. The second accesses the sound form (or the *phonological* form) of the familiar written word directly from print. The third uses knowledge of common mappings between graphemes and phonemes to pronounce unfamiliar written stimuli.

This short survey of the stimuli used in studies of reading does not do justice to the full range of characteristics of the reading stimuli available. For example, regular words can vary in their degree of regularity; nonsense words can be made more or less difficult by varying their similarity to real words; words may be more or less frequent; and the meaning of words may be more or less concrete. All these properties can be shown to have an effect upon reading. These aspects are not essential players in the discussion presented here, but they will appear in the content of the book where more subtle arguments are made.

MODELS OF READING

Like most theories in psychology, those put forward to account for reading are controversial, and it is in this controversy that much of the interest in the study of reading lies. At present, there are two main theoretical accounts of the normal reading system: the two-route model (Coltheart, Curtis, Atkins, & Haller, 1993) and the triangle model (Plaut, 1997; Plaut, McClelland, Seidenberg, & Patterson, 1996; Seidenberg & McClelland, 1989).[1] These accounts are explained clearly by Andrew Ellis et al. in Chapter 4. However, since their account comes relatively late in the book, a brief description of these two theories will be given here, drawing upon their terminology and illustrations.

It was noted in the preceding section that studies of reading performance using different types of stimuli appear to require three procedures. The first is a procedure for pronouncing novel words and nonwords using the most common mappings between letters and sounds. The second, is a procedure for mapping familiar written words directly onto their corresponding

---

[1] A further connectionist model proposed by Zorzi, Houghton, and Butterworth (1998) has been published since this chapter was written. This model differs from previous distributed connectionist models by the addition of a sub-lexical pathway that assembles spelling–sound mappings from training on a word set that includes many irregular words.

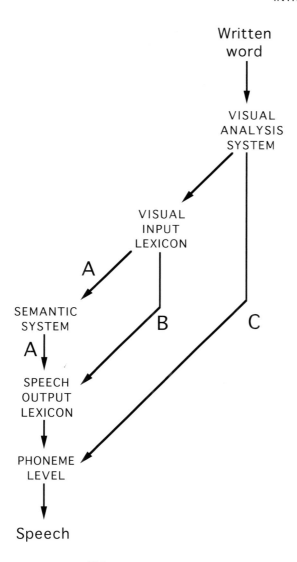

FIG. 1   The dual-route model.

phonological forms; and the third is a procedure for mapping a written word directly onto its meaning. The two-route model and the triangle model offer different accounts of how these procedures are aligned.

The two-route model links the two lexical processes together, and separates these distinctly from sub-lexical processes (Fig. 1). Familiar written words are recognised by activity in the written word-form system (referred to here as the visual input lexicon). Two separate lexical pathways link the visual input lexicon to the speech output lexicon in which the spoken word forms are stored. Pathway A passes through the semantic system where word meanings are stored before accessing the speech output lexicon. This pathway would enable the meaning of isolated written homophones, such as *pare* to be understood. In contrast, Pathway B links the visual input lexicon directly to the speech output lexicon. Pathway C maps graphemes onto phonemes and allows unfamiliar written words that are not represented in the visual input lexicon to be pronounced. Success in deriving a correct pronunciation of a word via pathway C will depend on whether or not the word is composed of regular grapheme–phoneme correspondences.

The main competitor to the dual-route model is the triangle model illustrated in Fig. 2. This model was put forward originally as a model of learning to read. Unlike the dual-route model there are no separable lexical components dedicated to the processing of familiar written and spoken word forms. Instead, an orthographic system processes representations of familiar and unfamiliar written words across sets of units representing graphemes; and a phonological system processes familiar and unfamiliar spoken words across sets of units representing phonemes. Thus, lexical and sub-lexical processes are superimposed across a single hardware. In this way, the triangle model avoids the problem of integrating new words into the lexical system. Two pathways connect the orthographic system with the phonological system: Pathway B links these two systems directly, whereas Pathway A

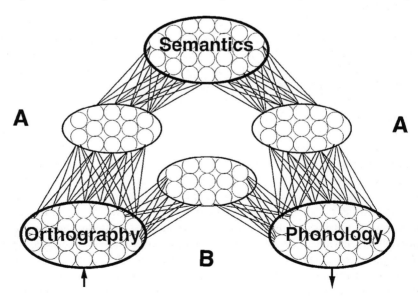

FIG. 2   The triangle model (reproduced with permission from Plaut, 1997).

connects orthographic and phonological representations of words with the semantic system, allowing written words to be understood directly from print. However, so far, only Pathway B has been fully simulated in a working model.

READING ERRORS

A "tool of the trade"—particularly important to the classification of reading disorders—is the reading error. Errors provide telling signs of the processes that are available for reading and those that have been impaired or failed to develop, and they play an important role in the development of theories of reading. Two principal types of reading error will be mentioned here.

The first is the *regularisation* error. Here, an irregular word is mispronounced using regular written-to-sound mappings. For example, the word *pint* may be pronounced to rhyme with "mint". Normal readers tend to make such errors when irregular words lie outside their reading vocabulary. For example, on the National Adult Reading Test, normal adult readers will often pronounce *deny* as "denny", *depot* as "deepot", and *courteous* as "corteous". These mistakes reflect an appropriate use of sub-lexical processes in an attempt to pronounce unfamiliar written words.

The second is the *semantic* error. Here, the subject gives a response that is related in meaning to the stimulus word, but which bears little orthographic relationship to the written form. For example, the word *tartan* may be read as "kilt". Such errors suggest that the relationship between the orthography and the phonology of the word form has been ignored, and the reading response has been based entirely on processes based on word meaning (which are not operating normally and so give rise to meaning-related errors). Such errors give further support to the theory that the reading system includes a lexical–semantic pathway which processes meaning directly from print.

These two errors—the regularisation error and the semantic error—are fundamental to understanding the processes available to subjects with reading disorders. A further error, the so-called "visual" error, also occurs commonly. Here, a word of similar orthographic form, but unrelated in meaning, is given as a response to a word. For example, the word *charm* may be read as "chair". Sometimes errors may be visually and semantically related to a word, as in the example *shade* read as "shadow". In acquired disorders of reading, visual errors are thought to arise when the meaning of the target word is not accessible and the meaning of a close orthographic neighbour is retrieved instead (see Chapter 2). Visual errors tend to occur when sub-lexical reading processes are either unavailable or not applied.

TYPES OF DYSLEXIA AND READING ERRORS

Acquired forms of dyslexia are usually divided into two broad classes: *peripheral* and *central* dyslexia. There are three types of peripheral dyslexia—pure alexia, neglect dyslexia, and simultanagnosia. Of these, *pure alexia* provides most information about the reading system; the other two forms reflect deficits to attentional mechanisms. Pure alexia arises from damage to posterior regions of the brain that disconnects the major pathways that link the visual areas involved in recognising written words with the more anterior language areas involved in comprehending and pronouncing words. The three central forms of acquired dyslexia are *deep*, *phonological*, and *surface* dyslexia. These central disorders arise from damage to language processes situated in the posterior areas of the temporal lobe and the angular gyrus of the hemisphere that is dominant for language (in most cases the left cerebral hemisphere). Functional brain imaging studies should help to elucidate the brain areas affected in particular reading disorders. Reports of functional imaging studies of pure and deep dyslexia can be found in Chapters 2 and 3.

Developmental forms of the acquired peripheral dyslexias do not appear to occur, but visual processing disorders are implicated in some cases of developmental dyslexia (Willows, Kruk, & Corcos, 1993). Reports of developmental forms of the central dyslexias of phonological dyslexia and surface dyslexia occur quite often; in contrast, cases of developmental deep dyslexia are very rare. At present, the aetiology of developmental reading disorders is not well understood.

Four types of acquired dyslexia—pure alexia, deep dyslexia, phonological dyslexia and surface dyslexia—will be presented in the first four chapters of this book. Developmental surface dyslexia will be presented in the final chapter. As a brief introduction, the principal characteristics of each disorder in relation to particular types of stimuli and particular types of reading error will be presented here. However, it is important to bear in mind that the characteristics referred to in the written outlines that follow, capture only the basic elements shared by most subjects described as having the disorder. There can be considerable variation in the degree to which particular characteristics appear in individuals.

Pure alexia

Subjects with pure alexia make none of the reading errors mentioned earlier. Instead, the most marked characteristics of this reading disorder is a tendency to name aloud the alphabetic letters in the written word. The letter names are then used as a basis for pronouncing the word. As a result of this strategy, words with more letters take longer to read, showing a characteristic effect of word length. As Saffran and Coslett explain in Chapter 1, this strategy appears to be used when the written word is not recognised overtly, and when grapheme–phoneme correspondences are not directly available. It is generally assumed from this that subjects with pure alexia do not have *direct* visual access to the normal reading system and that letter naming allows letter information to access the reading system by other routes. Of great theoretical interest, however, is the fact that some subjects appear to have fast access to written word recognition processes of which they are unaware. To expose this "implicit" reading process, Saffran and Coslett show that it is necessary to persuade the subjects to "turn off" the letter-by-letter strategy and make decisions on the basis of an impression of the word and its meaning. When this is successful, subjects appear to be able to process the broad semantic category to which the word belongs, even when the word is presented for a time that is too short for explicit word recognition and naming. This implicit reading system is argued to reside in the right cerebral hemisphere. The letter-by-letter reading strategy is thought to be a left hemisphere process.

Deep dyslexia

Deep dyslexic subjects make semantic errors (and usually visual errors too). In most cases the ability to pronounce written nonwords is abolished, indicating an impairment to sub-lexical processing skills. In addition, deep dyslexic subjects do not make regularisation errors to unfamiliar irregular words. Success with reading words aloud is restricted mainly to concrete content words such as *house*, *walk*, *quiet*, that have specific referential meaning. Abstract words, such as *idea*, *truth*, *pride*, are much less likely to be read aloud successfully. Function words, such as *was*, *then*, *because*, which serve a purely grammatical purpose, tend to be read very poorly or not at all, even though subjects recognise the visual forms of these words as familiar. This word-class effect suggests that the direct pathway, which would process familiar written word forms of all types, is impaired; as too must be the sub-lexical pathway. Instead, reading in deep dyslexia is limited to the reading of meaningful words, indicating a reliance on the lexical–semantic pathway. This is supported by the incidence of semantic errors.

It has proved difficult to explain the pattern of characteristics of deep dyslexia within a model of normal reading. One solution (supported by evidence of widespread left hemisphere damage in deep dyslexia) has been to argue that deep dyslexia reflects the activity of right hemisphere processes, not normally involved in reading. Chapter 2 reviews recent brain imaging studies of written word processing in deep dyslexia and concludes that these provide little support for the right hemisphere hypothesis. The contribution of computer simulations of deep dyslexia, which have been able to reproduce semantic and visual-semantic errors and differences between concrete and abstract words, are also reviewed. The chapter closes with the discussion of a proposal that, in deep dyslexic subjects, single written word reference tasks call up processes normally dedicated to object naming (see Chapter 1 for a similar argument).

Phonological dyslexia

Subjects with phonological dyslexia show a marked contrast between their ability to read words and nonwords. In the most impaired cases, the subjects are unable to pronounce written nonwords aloud. In addition, they do not regularise the pronunciation of unfamiliar irregular words (e.g. they do not read the word *pint* to rhyme with "mint"), and they do not read regular words more successfully than irregular words when these words are matched for frequency. Their most characteristic error is the visual error, in which they produce a word orthographically similar to the stimulus. Unlike subjects with deep dyslexia, they rarely, if ever, make semantic errors, and any difference observed between the reading of content and function words tends to be slight compared with the disparity observed in deep dyslexia. The classic explanation of phonological dyslexia (in both acquired and developmental cases) is a dependence upon lexical processes in the face of impoverished or absent sub-lexical skills.

Phonological dyslexia has been a "thorn in the flesh" of the triangle model, which has had difficulty explaining how damage to the direct ortho-graphic–phonological reading route could spare word reading relative to nonwords. In a thought-provoking study, reported in Chapter 3, Karalyn Patterson broadens the study of phonological dyslexia to investigate the contribution of phonological deficits to tasks such as blending, rhyming, and phoneme segmentation, involving language processes extending beyond the processes dedicated to reading. She also investigates the possibility that in some cases of phonological dyslexia, reading depends upon the lexical semantic pathway. She presents an in-depth study of a single subject using a variety of innovative methods and concludes that the subject's pattern of deficits can be explained as a dependence upon lexical semantic processing within the triangle model of reading.

Surface dyslexia

In contrast to deep and phonological dyslexia (in which lexical reading is superior to sub-lexical reading), *surface* dyslexia is thought to arise when sub-lexical skills overcompensate for impoverished lexical skills. A previously skilled adult reader, with an acquired form of surface dyslexia, may fail to recognise previously familiar written words and attempt instead to sound out the words using sub-lexical processes. So long as the sub-lexical processes are working normally, regular words will be pronounced correctly, and the irregular words that the subject fails to recognise will be regularised. Thus, a regularity effect, favouring the pronunciation of regular words relative to irregular words, is a characteristic of surface dyslexia.

In Chapter 4, Andrew Ellis et al. elaborate on this simple explanation by distinguishing three types of surface dyslexia with deficits occurring in different parts of the reading system: input; central (semantic); and output; and provides case-study illustrations of each. A successful therapy programme is described based on an understanding of the type of surface dyslexic disorder the subject was experiencing. Both dual-route and triangle models of normal reading need to be able to give satisfactory accounts of the three types of surface dyslexia. These models are investigated in turn through the detailed analysis and application of individual cases of surface dyslexia. As Ellis et al. acknowledge, not all aspects of the cases can be satisfactorily explained, particularly within the triangle model. One possible reason for this is that some cases may have developed idiosyncratic reading processes before brain damage.

Developmental dyslexia

It was mentioned earlier that cases of developmental dyslexia have been described that have the characteristics of either acquired phonological or surface dyslexia. That is, children have been reported who have particular difficulty with either sub-lexical or lexical processing. Children with *developmental phonological dyslexia* have particular problems sounding out unfamiliar words and nonwords using sub-lexical processes and tend to rely instead on the recognition of familiar written words for reading. Children with *surface dyslexia* have particular problems building a lexical vocabulary of familiar written words, and tend to rely instead on sub-lexical processes for achieving a pronunciation. When these children were first described it was argued that they had failed to develop particular skills because of under-lying processing deficits. This conclusion has been the source of some controversy.

One early criticism was that the patterns of performance found in developmental surface dyslexia and phonological dyslexia can be observed in normal readers at an earlier stage of reading development, indicating that the characteristics of different forms of developmental dyslexia do not, of themselves, signify a fundamental processing deficit. A second early criticism was that no yardstick had been used for measuring the degree of impairment to the lexical and sub-lexical processing skills. An inspection of the early cases of phonological and surface dyslexia suggested that the children appeared to have impairments to both lexical and sub-lexical processes with relatively greater impairments in one skill compared with another. In Chapter 5, Jackie Masterson addresses these issues. She introduces studies that have developed methods for determining deficient levels of processing relative to the norm and discusses further case reports of developmental surface dyslexia in English, Italian, and Spanish children. Experimental techniques, developed to investigate factors that might hinder the development of lexical processes, are also described. She concludes that there are indications in the literature that at least some children with surface dyslexia have abnormal strategies for processing print. Although her discussion focuses on developmental surface dyslexia, many of the studies referred to, and many of the points made, apply equally to developmental phonological dyslexia.

REFERENCES

Coltheart, M., Curtis, B., Atkins, P., & Haller, M. (1993). Models of reading aloud: Dual-route and parallel-distributed-processing approaches. *Psychological Review, 100,* 589–608.

Ellis, A.W. (1993). *Reading, writing and dyslexia (*2nd ed.). Hove, UK: Lawrence Erlbaum Associates Ltd.

Plaut, D. (1997). Structure and function in the lexical system: Insights from distributed models of word reading and lexical decision. *Language and Cognitive Processes, 12,* 767–808.

Plaut, D.C., McClelland, J.L., Seidenberg, M.S., & Patterson, K. (1996). Understanding normal and impaired word reading: Computational principles in quasi-regular domains. *Psychological Review, 103,* 56–115.

Seidenberg, M.S., & McClelland, J.L. (1989). A distributed, developmental model of word recognition and naming. *Psychological Review, 97,* 447–452.

Willows, D.M., Kruk, R.S., & Corcos, E. (1993). *Visual processes in reading and reading disabilities.* Hillsdale, NJ: Lawrence Erlbaum Associates Inc.

Zorzi, M., Houghton, G., & Butterworth, B. (1998). Two routes or one in reading aloud? A connectionist dual-process model. *Journal of Experimental Psychology: Human Perception and Performance, 24,* 1131–1161.

CHAPTER ONE

Pure alexia: The case of JG

Eleanor M. Saffran
Temple University School of Medicine, Philadelphia, USA

H. Branch Coslett
Temple University School of Medicine, Philadelphia, USA

One of the remarkable results of brain damage is the syndrome known as
pure alexia, or alexia without agraphia—the inability to read in the context
of preserved writing and spelling, including material the patient has written.
The dissociation between reading and writing was first described by
Déjerine (1892) in a patient who had suffered an infarction of the left occipital cortex and portions of the splenium of the corpus callosum. Déjerine
accounted for this unusual pattern in terms of a disconnection between visual
input and mechanisms for recognising printed words. He suggested that the
left occipital lesion not only restricts visual processing to the right hemisphere but also prevents visual information from reaching the repository of
word forms ("optical images of letters"), which he located in the left
angular gyrus. More recently, the severity of the reading deficit in pure
alexia provided the basis for Geschwind's (1965) claim that the right hemisphere is word-blind.

Unable to read in the usual sense, most patients with pure alexia compen-
sate by identifying words letter by letter. This laborious process is evident in
the overt production of letter names, which is often transitory, as well as an
effect of word length on reading time. The latter effect is taken to be the
signature of letter-by-letter reading. Other features of the syndrome include
letter identification errors, which appear to reflect confusions based on
visual similarity (upper case C might be identified as G), and greater difficulty reading cursive writing than print (e.g. Warrington & Shallice, 1980).

Most recent accounts of pure alexia have emphasised difficulty in letter
recognition as the basis for the reading deficit (e.g. Arguin & Bub, 1993,
1994; Behrmann & Shallice, 1995; Reuter-Lorenz & Brunn, 1990). Other
proposals include damage to the word-form system (Warrington & Shallice,
1980), attentional impairment (Rapp & Caramazza, 1991), and a perceptual
deficit that is not specific to alphabetic materials (e.g. Farah & Wallace,

1991; Kinsbourne & Warrington, 1962). In our view, the evidence for an impairment in letter recognition is compelling. But the explanatory problem does not end here. Interpretation of the deficit pattern is complicated by the fact that some pure alexics retain the ability to access word forms rapidly—as indexed, for example, by their performance on lexical decision tasks—although this capacity usually does not support explicit identification of the word. Evidence for "implicit" word recognition in pure alexics is difficult to reconcile with a problem in letter recognition, or indeed with any of the other accounts mentioned earlier.

Reports of some capacity for word recognition in pure alexia began to appear in the 1970s (Albert, Yamadori, Gardner, & Howes, 1973; Caplan & Hedley-Whyte, 1974; Landis, Regard, & Serrat, 1980). In 1986, Shallice and Saffran carried out the first detailed examination of this phenomenon. They reported a case study of a patient, ML, who displayed all of the characteristics of alexia without agraphia and letter-by-letter reading. When words were presented at exposures too brief to allow them to be identified letter-by-letter, ML proved to be able to perform lexical decision and semantic categorization tasks at above-chance levels. Although these tasks clearly entailed word recognition, ML was rarely able to identify the letter strings explicitly. On occasion, he would supply some information about the meaning of the word (e.g. for *dinner*, "food ... meal-time kind of thing"). Another striking feature of his performance was that he did not take full advantage of the 2 seconds allowed him under the limited exposure condition. Instead, he would glance briefly at the stimulus and look away, a behaviour pattern that suggested an attempt to inhibit letter-by-letter reading by reducing exposure to the letter string.

Other demonstrations of "implicit" reading on the part of pure alexics were soon forthcoming (e.g. Bub, Black, & Howell, 1989; Feinberg, Dyckes-Berke, Miner, & Roane, 1995;[1] Howard, 1990). In this chapter, we describe one such example—the case of JG (Coslett & Monsul, 1994; Coslett & Saffran, 1989a, 1994). We provide an account of both facets of his performance, the alexia manifested under standard testing conditions as well as the ability to read "implicitly".

CASE HISTORY

JG is a right-handed former meat salesman with a high-school education. At the age of 53, he suddenly had difficulty reading road signs and noted an inability to see on the right while driving. He also found that he was unable

---

[1] Feinberg et al. have shown that a pure alexic patient was able to give confidence ratings for words she failed to identify explicitly. On those grounds, they argue that the patient's performance reflects "partial" rather than "implicit" knowledge.

to remember frequently used telephone numbers. These symptoms persisted, and he sought medical attention the following day. Upon admission, he was found to have a dense right homonymous hemianopia, impaired memory function, moderate anomia, and severe alexia. CT and MRI scans revealed small areas of infarction in the area of the left lateral geniculate and the splenium of the corpus callosum, as well as a small infarct in the left frontal lobe. The left occipital, temporal, and parietal areas appeared normal. An MRI obtained 4 years later showed dilatation of the left temporal horn that was not present initially, the result of degeneration that occurred subsequent to the lateral geniculate lesion.

On a neuropsychological evaluation conducted 5 weeks after the stroke, JG demonstrated a moderate degree of anomia, with particular difficulty in colour naming. When examined more extensively 2 months post-onset, testing with the Boston Diagnostic Aphasia Examination revealed no evidence of aphasia. However, a mild naming deficit was apparent on the Boston Naming Test, where JG correctly identified 43/60 items, and an additional 5 with a phonological cue. At this point, he had no difficulty naming or pointing to named colours. The memory deficit that was initially apparent had also resolved.

The patient's spelling and writing abilities were judged to be appropriate for his level of education. He wrote correctly 38/40 regular and 35/40 irregular words, matched for length and frequency, and was 14/15 correct in writing nonwords. He identified 35/40 regular and 34/40 irregular words spelled aloud by the examiner.

In naming letters, JG was slow and prone to error. When presented with single lower case letters, he identified 23/26 correctly, but generally made several attempts before producing the correct name. In identifying letters in words, he responded incorrectly on 20% of the trials.

Initially, JG appeared to be unable to read except by using a letter-by-letter strategy. His performance showed the usual relationship between word length and reading time (Fig. 1.1), but no effect of variables such as orthographic regularity, imageability, or part of speech. Thus, he read 36/39 regular and 35/39 irregular words, 28/30 nouns and 27/30 functors; for both comparisons, the materials were matched for length and frequency. He also read 40/40 nonwords correctly. In most cases, his errors appeared to reflect letter misidentifications; for example, he read *marker* as "market" and *match* as "march".

The first set of studies on JG was conducted over a period of 8 months; he was also tested again 3 years later. Three months post-onset, the dense right homonymous hemianopia that was present initially had partially resolved. JG detected movement and could see what he described as "outlines" or silhouettes in the right visual field, although he appeared unable to read or to identify letters or small objects. These capacities were

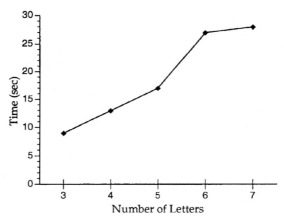

FIG. 1.1   Mean reading time for words read correctly as a function of word length in JG.

further tested under tachistoscopic conditions, using short presentation times (50–150msec) to preclude eye movements. JG showed no evidence of ability to discriminate words from nonwords in the right visual field (RVF), although he did demonstrate such sensitivity in the left visual field (LVF), performing 85% correct on a lexical decision task with LVF presentation. These data argue against left hemisphere mediation of the "implicit" reading capacities described in more detail below.

EVIDENCE FOR IMPLICIT READING

JG was the first of a series of patients tested in our lab on the types of tasks that Shallice and Saffran (1986) had used to demonstrate the preservation of reading capacities in ML. These included lexical decision and categorisation tasks, in which stimuli were presented too briefly to allow effective use of letter-by-letter reading. It should be stated at the outset that JG, like other pure alexics tested in this fashion, initially protested that he could not read at all under these conditions. Indeed, he could not, if reading is defined as involving explicit report of the stimulus. Only after repeated successes on the tasks described below did he reluctantly concede that he could even "see" the entire letter string.

Lexical decision

The first task that we used to explore implicit reading capacity was lexical decision—determining whether or not a letter string was an English word. When we first began to test him, JG, like other such patients, had a strong tendency to apply the letter-by-letter reading strategy, even though he was unable to report more than one or two letters under the brief exposure condition. To discourage such attempts, JG was told that it was not necessary to report the letter string, but simply to indicate whether it was a word or not. He was instructed to get a "feeling" for or "impression" of the stimulus, and to guess when he was uncertain. Only when he believed that he had recognised the word was he to report it.

The stimuli included 60 high frequency and 60 low frequency words, 60 nonwords with common English orthographic patterns (e.g. *shart*) and 60 with unusual or illegal letter combinations (e.g. *twilk*). Stimuli were matched for length (three–five letters) across conditions and presented on a computer screen for 250msec.

JG's performance is summarised in Table 1.1. It is evident that he was sensitive to the lexicality of the letter strings, at least for high frequency words. To rule out the possibility that he was responding to orthographic familiarity rather than lexical status, we carried out a post hoc analysis that controlled for orthographic factors. We did this by selecting a sub-set of the materials in which the frequency of letter combinations ("N"; see Coltheart, Davelaar, Jonasson, & Besner, 1977) was equated across words and nonwords. The results of this analysis (Table 1.1) establish that JG was responding on the basis of the lexical status of the string, and not its orthographic characteristics.

To examine JG's performance as a function of presentation time, the same stimuli were presented on several occasions at different exposures (Table 1.2). Although his responses were most accurate with unlimited presentation, which allowed him to read letter by letter, he actually did better at shorter exposure times, discriminating words at above-chance levels, than at

TABLE 1.1
JG's performance on lexical decision (250msec)

	"Yes" Responses (%)
Words	
High Frequency	75
Low Frequency	37
Both	56
High N	63
Low N	55
Nonwords	
Common	35
Unusual	25
Both	30
High N	33
Low N	28

N refers to the frequency of occurrence of letter combinations. For example, "Shart" would be a Hi-N nonword, whereas "twilk" would be a Lo-N nonword.

TABLE 1.2
JG's lexical decision performance as a function of exposure duration, in "Yes" responses (%)

Exposure	50msec	250msec	500msec	2000msec	Unlimited
Words	49	59	55	51	86
High Frequency	57	68	70	64	
Low Frequency	40	57	40	37	
Nonwords	22	36	21	54	8
High N	27	33	25	68	
Low N	18	28	18	40	
d'	0.75	0.72	0.93	0.13	2.49

N refers to the frequency of occurrence of letter combinations. For example, "Shart" would be a Hi-N nonword, whereas "twilk" would be a Lo-N nonword.

2sec, where his performance was at chance. Presumably, the 2sec exposure was long enough to engage the letter-by-letter strategy, but not long enough to permit identification of enough letters to specify the word.

Categorisation

JG's ability to extract semantic information from rapidly presented words was examined in three tasks. The first required him to determine whether the word signified an animal (e.g. *mouse*); the second, whether it was a type of food (e.g. *grape*). The two tasks employed the same design: 25 target words (animals in the first, food in the second), 25 words that were orthographically similar to targets (e.g. *mount* in the animal set, *graph* in the food set), and 25 words that bore no orthographic similarity to animal or food words. JG's third task was to decide whether a letter string represented a male (e.g. *Maurice*) or a female name (e.g. *Maureen*). Again, he was encouraged to get a "feeling for" or "impression" of the stimulus, and only to report the word when he was sure he had recognised it.

The results of these experiments are summarised in Table 1.3. As in the case of lexical decision, JG's performance was far from perfect but significantly better than chance.

Word–picture matching

In this task, JG was required to match a rapidly presented word to one of two pictures that were presented after the word had disappeared. Two sets of materials were administered: the foil was from a different category than the target (n = 62) in one set and was a category co-ordinate in the other (n

TABLE 1.3
JG's performance on categorisation tests (percentage correct)

	Performance (% correct)
Animal	80
Visual foil	72
Unrelated foil	72
Total	75
Food	84
Visual foil	76
Unrelated foil	80
Total	80
Names	–
Male	74
Female	76
Total	75

= 30). In the first set, the target and the foil shared at least the first two letters (e.g. *house*, *horse*); in the second set, they shared at least the initial letter (e.g. *snake*, *spider*). Each word in the pair was tested separately. For this task, the words were exposed for 500msec. JG was correct on 87% of the cross-category and 90% of the within-category trials.

Explicit word identification

On the tasks described previously, which were administered between 2 and 4 months after his stroke, JG provided an explicit response on approximately 5% of the trials. Although these responses generally bore some orthographic similarity to the target (e.g. *alliance* → "alligator"), they were generally incorrect. In a few cases, he provided some semantic information about the word although he was unable to name it (e.g. for *saddle*, "connected to horse", for *canoe*, "ride in water"). Over the ensuing months, JG showed an increasing ability to explicitly identify words under tachistoscopic conditions. His performance under these conditions differed in two respects from his performance with unlimited exposure: He was less accurate overall, and his accuracy differed across types of words. With brief exposure, JG showed word class and imageability effects that did not emerge when he was reading letter by letter.

Tested 6 months post-onset at 250msec exposure with 30 nouns and 30 function words matched for length and frequency, JG was 77% correct on nouns and only 47% correct on functors. Presented with 40 high and 40 low imageability nouns, matched in length and frequency, JG read 88% of the high and 63% of the low imageability nouns correctly. In both cases, these differences were statistically significant. His ability to read closed-class morphemes was further tested by contrasting inflected words (e.g. *flowed*) with "pseudo-inflected" words (e.g. *flower*). Forty such pairs were generated, in which the two members of the pair were approximately matched for frequency. Again, the stimuli were presented for 250msec. JG was 30% correct on the suffixed set and 73% correct on the pseudosuffixed set, again a significant difference. The same pattern emerged in two other recovering alexic patients that we tested (Coslett & Saffran, 1989a).

DISCUSSION

We have, then, a situation in which a patient is (at least initially) able to identify printed words only by means of a laborious procedure that involves sequential letter identification, yet at the same time shows clear evidence of the ability to process letter strings rapidly and in parallel—but apparently (at least at first) without explicit knowledge of the word. As previously noted, JG is not the only pure alexic to demonstrate this pattern. Our investigation of JG was modelled on Shallice and Saffran's (1986) demonstration of a very similar pattern in ML, and we have obtained comparable effects in other pure alexics studied in our laboratory (Coslett & Saffran, 1989a, 1994). Two of the patients we have investigated manifested pure alexia in the context of a severe optic aphasia, a disorder in which patients are unable to name objects presented visually, although they can name them to tactile presentation and to definition. The two optic aphasics were completely unable to read words aloud, or to name visually presented letters; nevertheless, both showed evidence of implicit reading in lexical decision and categorisation tasks (Coslett & Saffran, 1989b, 1992). Of four alexics who were also letter-by-letter readers, two showed recovery patterns similar to that of JG—an increasing ability to identify letter strings at short presentations that was biased toward concrete words (Coslett & Saffran, 1989a, Cases 2 and 3). Of the two alexics who did not show this pattern, one had extensive brain damage (Coslett & Saffran, 1989a, Case 4) and the other declined further testing (Coslett, Saffran, Greenbaum, & Schwartz, 1993). The same pattern has also been demonstrated in a partially recovered alexic recently studied by Buxbaum and Coslett (1996). This patient (JH) showed the effect of word length that typifies letter-by-letter reading, but only for low imageability words. Although JH had to resort to the letter-by-letter procedure for low imageability words, he was able to employ parallel processing to identify high imageability words.

Other investigators have obtained additional forms of evidence for rapid processing of letter strings in patients characterised as letter-by-letter readers. For example, Howard (1990) found that a pure alexic patient was sensitive to a briefly presented biasing cue (e.g. *angry* or *church*) when the

task was to define an ambiguous target word (e.g. *cross*). Several investigators (Bub et al., 1989; Reuter-Lorenz & Brunn, 1990) have demonstrated
word superiority effects (superior letter identification in words as compared
with unrelated letter strings) in letter-by-letter readers. Performance did not
decline across letter positions in identifying letters within words, as one
might expect if the patient was reading letter by letter; this effect did emerge
with strings of unrelated letters. Other relevant evidence comes from studies
of number processing in pure alexics. Whereas the ability to name numbers
and to carry out arithmetic operations is impaired, comprehension of
numbers, as indicated by appreciation of their magnitude, is preserved
(Cohen & Dehaene, 1995).

All of the pure alexics who have been tested for implicit reading ability in
our laboratory ($n = 8$) have demonstrated the effect. Other investigators
have reported negative results, possibly because they did not do enough to
discourage their patients from reading letter by letter. For example,
Patterson & Kay (1982) asked two alexic patients to perform lexical decision, but only after an attempt at reporting the target. As noted earlier, JG's
performance on the lexical decision task declined when exposure time was
increased to 2 seconds, which was long enough to encourage an attempt at
the letter-by-letter approach but not long enough to implement it successfully. An explicit demonstration of the incompatibility of the two types of
reading was provided by Coslett et al. (1993). The patient, JWC, performed
well on categorisation tasks with briefly presented (249msec) stimuli, until
an explicit reading task, with unlimited exposure, was interpolated.
Following this, he performed at chance in categorising words presented at
2000msec that he was instructed first to name. His categorisation performance improved again when exposure was reduced to 249msec. Thus it
appears that access to information that becomes available in implicit reading
tasks may be blocked when the patient is reading letter by letter. This possibility was also suggested by the behaviour of Shallice & Saffran's (1986)
patient ML, who deliberately cut short the stimulus exposure allowed him in
implicit reading tasks. Although it is possible that the capacity to process
letter strings in parallel is limited to a sub-set of pure alexics (see e.g.
Howard, 1990), we reserve judgement on this issue. To demonstrate the
effect, it appears that it will be necessary to actively discourage patients'
attempts to read letter by letter.

In any event, it is clear that some pure alexics do have the capacity to
process letter strings rapidly and that this capacity requires explanation. One
possible account of this phenomenon is that it reflects weak activation of the
system that normally subserves explicit word identification: "Weak input
from an impaired word-form system could allow sufficient activation of the
corresponding semantic representation to activate other representations by
spreading activation, but not enough to inhibit the competing possibilities

which explicit identification requires" (Shallice & Saffran, 1986, p. 452). Although this may be a reasonable explanation for implicit reading, it does not readily accommodate two other findings: (1) Words can be explicitly identified if they are read letter by letter. Why should letter-by-letter reading elicit a "stronger" response than apprehension of the letter string as a whole? (2) Word-class effects emerged in the recovered reading of JG and other pure alexics tested in our laboratory (Coslett & Saffran, 1989a). These effects suggest that explicit report via whole word reading is semantically mediated. Why should there be semantic dependency for whole word recognition but not for reading letter by letter?

One solution to the problem is to assume that different systems are responsible for the two types of reading performance. Let us first consider reading letter by letter. The slow, sequential nature of this process, coupled with the tendency toward letter identification errors that is observed in most, if not all, pure alexics, certainly suggests that these patients are not processing letters normally. Direct evidence to this effect has come from several studies. Arguin and Bub (1994; also see Kay & Hanley, 1991; Reuter-Lorenz & Brunn, 1990) found, for example, that a pure alexic patient was sensitive to identity priming in a letter naming task (e.g. where the upper case letter A preceded the target A), but not to physically different/name identical priming (e.g. a did not prime A). Normal subjects do show effects of name priming, which are presumably mediated by an abstract orthographic code in which a and A are equivalent. Arguin and Bub (1994, p. 266) conclude that "an encoding impairment of letters and words as abstract orthographic entities lies at the origin of the reading deficit". We concur with this view (Coslett & Saffran, 1994), but only with respect to explicit identification of words and letters. Insofar as implicit reading is concerned, it appears that letters are identified rapidly and in parallel. How do we resolve this disparity?

Our account is in some aspects similar to Déjerine's (1892). Due to the left occipital (or geniculate) lesion, visual input is processed in the right hemisphere. The lesion also prevents visual input from contacting the left hemisphere reading system in the normal manner, that is, on the basis of abstract letter identities, made available in parallel. We speculate that this is because the lesion blocks transfer of visual information to the left hemisphere in a form that provides access to the normal mechanisms for letter encoding (see Coslett & Saffran, 1994, for discussion). With the normal route inoperative, the alexic left hemisphere resorts to naming letters by means of processes that are used to identify and name other visual objects. These processes operate on one object at a time and are not optimal for word recognition. As letters are identified and named, they gain access to the orthographic lexicon by means of mechanisms normally employed in recognising words spelled orally—a capacity that is generally well-preserved in pure alexia. If this account is correct, the ability to read letter by letter should be linked to the ability to name objects presented visually. We note in this context that the two pure alexics we tested who could not name letters were profoundly optic aphasic; both patients were unable to name objects to visual presentation although they were able to name on the basis of tactile presentation or definition (Coslett & Saffran, 1989b, 1992).

If the left hemisphere is unable to identify letters in the normal manner, what is the basis for the implicit reading that occurs when letter strings are presented too rapidly to support explicit word identification? We have suggested that implicit reading, as well as the explicit reading that JG and other partially recovered pure alexics demonstrated under brief presentation, is the product of another set of reading mechanisms based in the right hemisphere. We invoke right hemisphere reading for several reasons. First, the processing of visual information is carried out by the right hemisphere in pure alexics. Second, the limitations of implicit reading performance in these patients bear a close similarity to reading patterns demonstrated by the isolated right hemisphere—in split-brain patients (e.g. Zaidel & Peters, 1981), in left hemispherectomy (Patterson, Vargha-Khadem, & Polkey 1989), and as tested by split field (LVF) presentation in a patient with a lesion of the posterior portion of the corpus callosum (Michel, Henaff, & Intrilligator, 1996). Specifically, the right hemisphere shows the bias towards high frequency words that is characteristic of the implicit reading performance of pure alexics; it also demonstrates the word-class effects that are evident in their recovered reading performance, as well as an apparent insensitivity to inflectional morphology. A further limitation of right hemisphere reading is an inability to encode printed words phonologically (Patterson et al., 1989; Zaidel & Peters, 1981); we have demonstrated the same limitation in one of our pure alexic patients who was also an optic aphasic (Coslett & Saffran, 1992). Finally, by making the reasonable assumption that the right hemisphere orthographic lexicon is less well elaborated than that of the left, we can also explain why the implicit reading performance of pure alexics is biased toward high frequency words (Coslett & Saffran, 1989a, 1994; Shallice & Saffran, 1986).

We have proposed, then, that the two reading mechanisms available to pure alexics reflect the involvement of two different reading systems. The first is the letter-by-letter strategy, which is engaged when the letter string remains in view for some period of time, and/or explicit report is required. This strategy entails letter recognition via object recognition procedures, and sequential input of letter information to the left hemisphere word-form system. It may be difficult to avoid engaging these left hemisphere systems when the task calls for an oral response. We suggest that implicit reading is subserved by another set of mechanisms in the right hemisphere that differ in certain respects from the reading and language capacities of the left.

One critical distinction between these two sets of reading capacities is that the left hemisphere mechanisms are an integral part of a system that controls language output whereas those that reside in the right hemisphere are not. A language production system is obliged to select single lexical items for output, and to do so rapidly and efficiently. The right hemisphere need not be subject to this constraint, and it appears that it is not. There is evidence, for example, that both senses of an ambiguous word remain active in the right hemisphere, whereas the left hemisphere rapidly suppresses the contextually inappropriate meaning (e.g. Faust & Gernsbacher, 1996). These and other findings have led to the speculation that the right hemisphere contributes to language processing tasks by activating a broader semantic field than the left (e.g. Beeman, Friedman, Grafman, Perez, Diamond, & Lindsay, 1994). A broad (or "coarsely coded") semantic representation could be useful in drawing inferences, interpreting metaphors, and maintaining coherence in discourse, all tasks in which patients with right hemisphere lesions are often deficient (see Beeman et al., 1994, for review). Since the right hemisphere does not translate graphemic input into phonological form (e.g. Zaidel & Peters, 1981), the information that it sends to the left hemisphere for phonological encoding is likely to be conceptual in nature. Lexicalisation of coarsely coded conceptual information could be problematic, particularly when the concepts are abstract in nature. Difficulty in translating the right hemisphere's coarsely coded semantic representation into a spoken word might explain the biases that are reflected in oral reading performance mediated, at least in part, by the right hemisphere—in cases of left hemispherectomy and posterior callosal lesions, and, we would argue, in the recovered whole word reading of patients like JG.

Although it should be possible to test the right hemisphere hypothesis by means of functional imaging techniques (PET or fMRI), we are not aware that any such study has been performed. Coslett & Monsul (1994) have taken a different approach to this question, using the technique of transcranial magnetic stimulation (TMS) to localise reading processes in JG. TMS involves the application of a magnetic field to the cranium, which interferes with underlying brain electrical activity. The study was carried out 8 years after his stroke. At that point, investigation of JG's reading revealed a pattern very similar to his performance 6 months post-onset. Tested with brief presentation (149msec), JG read approximately two-thirds of the words correctly, showing the same discrepancies between high and low imageability words and content and function words that he had demonstrated earlier. When TMS was applied to the left temporoparietal area, JG's performance was unaffected; he read 61% of words with stimulation and 68% without. In contrast, TMS had a significant effect when applied to the right temporoparietal area; JG was 21% correct with stimulation and 71% without. (The application of TMS had no effect on the reading of normal controls, who were performing at ceiling under these conditions.) Whereas these results are consistent with the right hemisphere hypothesis, they do not localise the disruption to a particular stage in the processing of printed words. However, as the stimulation was applied over temporoparietal cortex and did not have any apparent perceptual effects, it is unlikely that TMS was interfering with an early stage in the visual processing stream.

It appears, then, that the situation in alexia without agraphia is more complex than Déjerine (1892) originally supposed. For the patients, this additional complexity could be beneficial: they have residual reading capacities of which they may be unaware. For neuropsychology, the existence of these capacities is problematic. First, there is the matter of accounting for the co-occurrence of two very different types of reading performance: one, slow and inefficient, that yields verbal output, and a rapid one that generally does not support explicit identification of the word. Our solution to this problem is to assign these behaviours to two separate mechanisms, one localised to the left hemisphere and the other to the right hemisphere. Should this hypothesis turn out to be correct, it will be necessary to account for the differences between the two reading systems as well as for the transactions between them. There are questions, as well, for attempts to remediate the reading deficit in pure alexia. Should the focus be on increasing the efficiency of letter-by-letter reading (Arguin & Bub, 1994), or on increasing the accessibility of information that normally does not reach conscious awareness?

REFERENCES

Albert, M.L., Yamadori, A., Gardner, H., & Howes, D. (1973). Comprehension in alexia. *Brain, 96*, 317–328.

Arguin, M., & Bub, D. (1993). Single-character processing in a case of pure alexia. *Neuropsychologia, 31*, 435–458.

Arguin, M., & Bub, D. (1994). Pure alexia: Attempted rehabilitation and its implications for interpretation of the deficit. *Brain and Language, 47*, 233–268.

Beeman, M., Friedman, R.B., Grafman, J., Perez, E., Diamond, S., & Lindsay, M.B. (1994). Summation priming and coarse coding in the right hemisphere. *Journal of Cognitive Neuroscience, 6*, 26–45.

Behrmann, M., & Shallice, T. (1995). Pure alexia: A nonspatial visual disorder affecting letter activation. *Cognitive Neuropsychology, 12*, 409–454.

Bub, D., Black, S.E., & Howell, J. (1989). Word recognition and orthographic context effects in a letter-by-letter reader. *Brain and Language, 39*, 405–427.

Buxbaum, L., & Coslett, H.B. (1996). Deep dyslexic phenomena in a letter-by-letter reader. *Brain and Language, 54*, 136–167.

Caplan, L.R., & Hedley-Whyte, T. (1974). Cueing and memory dysfunction in alexia without agraphia: A case report. *Brain, 97*, 251–262.

Cohen, L., & Dehaene, S. (1995). Number processing in pure alexia: The effect of hemispheric asymmetries and task demands. *Neurocase, 1*, 121–137.

Coltheart, M., Davelaar, R.E., Jonasson, J.T., & Besner, D. (1977). Access to the internal lexicon. In S. Dornic (Ed.), *Attention and performance VI* (pp. 535–555). Hillsdale, NJ: Lawrence Erlbaum Associates Inc.

Coslett, H.B., & Monsul, N. (1994). Reading with the right hemisphere: Evidence from transcranial magnetic stimulation. *Brain and Language, 46,* 198–211.

Coslett, H.B., & Saffran, E.M. (1989a). Evidence for preserved reading in "pure alexia". *Brain, 112,* 327–359.

Coslett, H.B., & Saffran, E.M. (1989b). Preserved object recognition and reading comprehension in optic aphasia. *Brain, 112,* 1091–1110.

Coslett, H.B., & Saffran, E.M. (1992). Optic aphasia and the right hemisphere: A replication and extension. *Brain and Language, 43,* 148–161.

Coslett, H.B., & Saffran, E. M. (1994). Mechanisms of implicit reading in alexia. In M. Farah & G. Ratcliffe (Eds), *The neuropsychology of high-level vision* (pp. 299–330). Hillsdale, NJ: Lawrence Erlbaum Associates Inc.

Coslett, H.B., Saffran, E.M., Greenbaum, S., & Schwartz, H. (1993). Reading in pure alexia. *Brain, 116,* 21–37.

Déjerine, J. (1892). Contribution à l'étude anatomo-pathologique et clinique des différentes variétés de cecite-verbale. *Memoires de la Société de Biologie, 4,* 61–90.

Farah, M.J., & Wallace, M.A. (1991). Pure alexia as a visual impairment: A reconsideration. *Cognitive Neuropsychology, 8,* 313–334.

Faust, M.E., & Gernsbacher, M.A. (1996). Cerebral mechanisms for suppression of inappropriate information during sentence comprehension. *Brain and Language, 53,* 234–259.

Feinberg, T.E., Dyckes-Berke, D., Miner, C.R., & Roane, D.M. (1995). Knowledge, implicit knowledge and metaknowledge in visual agnosia and pure alexia. *Brain, 118,* 789–800.

Geschwind, N. (1965). Disconnexion syndromes in animals and man. *Brain, 88,* 588–644.

Howard, D. (1990). Letter-by-letter readers: Evidence for parallel processing. In D. Besner & G. Humphreys (Eds), *Basic processes in reading* (pp. 34–76). Hillsdale, NJ: Lawrence Erlbaum Associates Inc.

Kay, J., & Hanley, R. (1991). Simultaneous form perception and serial letter recognition in a case of letter-by-letter reading. *Cognitive Neuropsychology, 8,* 249–273.

Kinsbourne, M., & Warrington, E.K. (1962). A disorder of simultaneous form perception. *Brain, 85,* 461–486.

Landis, T., Regard, M., & Serrat, A. (1980). Iconic reading in a case of alexia without agraphia caused by a brain tumor: A tachistoscopic study. *Brain and Language, 11,* 45–53.

Michel, F., Henaff, M.-A., & Intrilligator, J. (1996). Two different readers in the same brain after a posterior callosal lesion. *Neuroreport, 7,* 786–788.

Patterson, K., Vargha-Khadem, F., & Polkey, C.F. (1989). Reading with one hemisphere. *Brain, 112,* 39–63.

Patterson, K.E., & Kay, J. (1982). Letter-by-letter reading: Psychological descriptions of a neurological syndrome. *Quarterly Journal of Experimental Psychology, 34A,* 411–441.

Rapp, B., & Caramazza, A. (1991). Spatially determined deficits in letter and word processing. *Cognitive Neuropsychology, 8,* 275–311.

Reuter-Lorenz, P.A., & Brunn, J.L. (1990). A prelexical basis for letter-by-letter reading: A case study. *Cognitive Neuropsychology, 7,* 1–20.

Shallice, T., & Saffran, E.M. (1986). Lexical processing in the absence of explicit word identification: Evidence from a letter-by-letter reader. *Cognitive Neuropsychology, 3,* 429–458.

Warrington, E.K., & Shallice, T. (1980). Word-form dyslexia. *Brain, 103,* 99–112.

Zaidel, E., & Peters. A.M. (1981). Phonological encoding and ideographic reading by the disconnected right hemisphere: Two case studies. *Brain and Language, 14,* 205–234.

CHAPTER TWO

Deep dyslexia

Elaine Funnell
Royal Holloway University of London, UK

INTRODUCTION

This chapter follows the fortunes, over more than three decades, of a classic case of deep dyslexia, and so provides a historical framework for this review of deep dyslexia. The chapter begins with a discussion of the characteristics of deep dyslexia, the way in which these have been refined, and their place within a model of normal reading. A discussion of computer simulations of deep dyslexia follows next. Then, a side-step into the right hemisphere hypothesis for deep dyslexia introduces evidence from functional imaging. The chapter closes with a discussion of the possibility that deep dyslexia taps into a system for nominal reference and considers the implications of this for the study of normal reading processes.

A CLASSIC CASE OF DEEP DYSLEXIA: GR

The classic case of deep dyslexia discussed in this chapter is GR, who was reported initially by Marshall and Newcombe in 1966. GR was not the first case of deep dyslexia to be reported; Coltheart (1980a) notes two earlier ones by Low (1931) and Goldstein (1948), but GR was the patient whose reading pattern catalysed the sudden flowering of interest in deep dyslexia that began in the 1970s and has continued over more than three decades.

Reports on GR appear at intervals over a period of 30 years, the different experiments in which he took part reflecting the developing theoretical questions directed towards deep dyslexia. Studies of other deep dyslexic subjects were reported also during this time, most notably KF (Shallice & Warrington, 1975) and PW and DE (Patterson, 1978, 1979; Patterson & Marcel, 1977), all of whom appear in various studies spanning several years.

GR made his debut into neuropsychological history in 1944. At this time he was 20 years old and a soldier on active service, when he accidentally shot himself as he fell from a lorry. The bullet entered his brain at a point just in front of his left ear and passed up through the temporal and parietal

27

lobes, damaging the sylvian fissure on the way, and emerging in the superior parietal region. He was found to have right-sided hemiplegia and a severe language disorder. At first, he was unable to produce words and could make only grunts with different inflections to communicate "yes" and "no". Subsequently, his spontaneous speech and comprehension improved, but persisting and severe difficulties with reading and writing remained.

More than 20 years later, GR's language abilities were re-assessed by John Marshall and Freda Newcombe (1966, 1973). They noted that GR's spontaneous speech generally lacked function words, giving it the quality of a telegram. However, his articulation was good and he could repeat single words, including foreign words, single phonemes, and numbers, but he found it difficult to recall series, such as the months of the year, and his digit span was reduced to three items only. Colours were difficult to name, although he was reported to name drawings of objects fairly well. His comprehension was generally good, but he found it difficult to follow instructions which used complex sentence structure.

GR's reading and spelling were severely affected. He could name only about half the letters of the alphabet and write about a third to dictation; but he could copy letters and transcribe from capital to lower case, and vice versa, showing that he recognised different forms of individual letters. Surprisingly, his success at reading written words aloud appeared to vary with the grammatical class of the word: he was most successful with nouns; less successful with adjectives; and had most problems with verbs (see Table 2.1). In addition, he read concrete nouns—referring to people, places, and things—more successfully than abstract nouns, indicating that his generally greater success with nouns varied with the nature of the reference of the word.

GR made a variety of reading errors that did not always preserve the grammatical form-class of the word. Although his errors to nouns were most often other nouns, his errors to adjectives were most likely also to be nouns. His errors to verbs were never other verbs but were either nouns or adjectives. He was virtually unable to read grammatical function words, such as prepositions, conjunctions, and pronouns, to which he substituted another function word: for example, he read *for* and *other* as "and"; and *her* and *his* as "she".

TABLE 2.1
Percentage of GR's oral reading of nouns, adjectives, and verbs

	Nouns (n=465)	Adjectives (n=197)	Verbs (n=284)
Correct	45	16	6
Fail to respond	19	47	65
Errors	36	37	29

Reproduced, with permission, from Marshall and Newcombe (1966).

The reading errors that GR made were revealing. His most common mistake was to produce a semantically related word. These errors shared some aspect of meaning with the target word but differed in orthographic or phonological form. For example, the written word *antique* was read as "vase". He made similar errors in spelling. These semantically related errors, which neither looked, nor sounded like the target word, suggested that the reading response was influenced by word meaning, rather than by the relationship between the written and spoken forms of the word.

Besides semantic errors, GR made so-called "visual" errors in which responses were related orthographically to the target word: for example, he read *deep* as "deer"; and *perform* as "perfume". A small sample of his errors were reported to be related orthographically and then semantically to the target. For example, he read *sympathy* as "orchestra", presumably by way of the visually related word "symphony". He also made a number of visual-completion errors such as beg→beggar; political→politician, which later came to be called "derivational errors". Derivational errors remove, add, or substitute a bound morpheme and, by so doing, change the meaning of the word.[1] Further examples of GR's reading errors are provided in Table 2.2.

TABLE 2.2
Examples of different types of reading errors made by GR

Error Types	Stimulus	Response
Semantic	antique	vase
	canary	parrot
	liberty	freedom
	gnome	pixie
Visual	deep	deer
	bad	bed
	shallow	sparrow
	wide	wisdom
Derivational	beg	beggar
	political	politician
	length	long
	heat	hot
Visual/semantic	sad	sack
	brass	band
	low	shallow
	young	strong
Visual then semantic	sympathy	orchestra
	earl	deaf
Function word substitutions	for	and
	her	she
	other	and
	his	she

[1] In contrast to derivational errors, changes to bound morphemes in inflectional errors affect the form of the word. For example, the tense of the word may change without changing the meaning. Inflectional errors are not a characteristic of deep dyslexia.

TABLE 2.3
Percentage of different error types occurring in GR's oral reading

	Nouns (n=169)	Adjectives (n=73)	Verbs (n=83)
Semantic	69.0	49.0	37.0
Visual	9.5	36.0	35.0
Visual/semantic	5.0	4.0	5.0
Derivational	9.5	5.5	18.0
Indeterminate	7.0	5.5	5.0

Interestingly, the proportion of semantic to visual errors differed according to the grammatical class of the word: semantic errors greatly outnumbered visual errors to nouns, only slightly outnumbering visual errors to adjectives, and producing equivalent levels to visual errors for verbs (see Table 2.3).

A THEORETICAL ACCOUNT OF GR'S ORAL READING

These early studies of GR's oral reading established two central characteristics of deep dyslexia: These were the effect of the grammatical class of words on reading success (shown later to be confounded with imageability); and the occurrence of semantic errors accompanied by visual and derivational errors and function word substitutions.

Parallels between the errors made in deep dyslexia and those found in normal reading were noted by Marshall and Newcombe (1973). They observed that semantic errors had also been reported in the reading of proficient normal adult readers when under time pressure, and in language tasks in which a memory component was introduced. Visual errors and grammatical word-class effects had been observed in studies in which words were presented visually for short time periods. These parallels between errors in deep dyslexia and those observed in studies of the performance of normal subjects, suggested to Marshall and Newcombe that the characteristics of deep dyslexia might be adequately accounted for within a model of normal reading.

The functional model of normal reading which Marshall and Newcombe (1973) put forward to account for deep dyslexia contained two pathways for oral reading. The first pathway, commonly referred to as the semantic pathway, processed whole written words and mapped these onto representations of word meaning. These were mapped in turn onto phonological addresses for spoken words. The second, sub-lexical, pathway parsed the words into letters and letter groups and mapped these onto their corresponding sounds (a process commonly referred to as grapheme–phoneme conversion). GR was thought to have lost the use of the sub-lexical pathway connecting graphemes with phonemes, so that he was forced to depend entirely for reading on the semantic pathway.[2]

GR's semantic errors were thought by Marshall and Newcombe (1966) to arise from a fault in the semantic pathway. Using the model of word meaning based on dictionary entries proposed by Katz and Fodor (1963), Marshall and Newcombe suggested that semantic errors would arise if only partial information in a dictionary entry was retrieved: For example, "tree" and "bush" would both be appropriate responses to the written word *bush* if the written word accessed only general information, such as "plant, with branches". They attributed the advantage for reading nouns to a proposal by Chomsky (1965) that nouns have priority in lexical selection.

The first direct evidence that deep dyslexic subjects lack the ability to convert graphemes to phonemes was obtained in nonword reading tasks carried out by Patterson and Marcel (1977). They studied two deep dyslexic subjects, DE (a young man who suffered brain injury in a motor scooter accident at the age of 16 years), and PW (an older man who had suffered a left hemisphere stroke when 57 years old). Neither subject was able to pronounce written nonwords or single letters even though they could repeat the spoken versions of the stimuli fairly well.

A further study conducted by Saffran and Marin (1977) showed that a deep dyslexic subject, VS, was unable to make judgements about the phonology of written material, even when the stimuli were words and no overt articulation was required. This subject, who suffered a stroke at the age of 48 years, could not carry out rhyming and homophone tasks with written words. She performed at chance level when asked to select one of four words to rhyme with a target word (e.g. to select a written word from *cuff, brought, cut, cough*, to rhyme with the written word *rough*), or to select a word which sounds the same as a target word (e.g. to select from *mayor, minor*, and *manner*, to match the target word *manor*). Her responses were based on the visual rather than the phonemic similarity of the words. So, in the examples given here, she selected the word *cough* to rhyme with *rough*, and *minor* to rhyme with *manor*. These studies, and many others conducted since, have supported the view that grapheme–phoneme conversion is abolished in deep dyslexia.

---

[2] In subsequent models, Morton and Patterson (1980a) added a further route to account for the oral reading of familiar words without access to semantic processing (see also, Coltheart, Curtis, Atkins, & Haller, 1993); Shallice and Warrington (1980) extended the direct sub-lexical route to process syllables and short words as well as grapheme–phoneme correspondences; and Seidenberg and McClelland (1989) combined the processing of familiar and unfamiliar words within a single distributed directed processing pathway. When accounting for the occurrence of deep dyslexia within each of these models the loss of the direct pathway, or pathways, is considered to be mandatory.

A SYNTHESIS OF FURTHER STUDIES

Studies of deep dyslexia blossomed over the decade following publication of Marshall and Newcombe's work and elaborated upon the properties of deep dyslexia which they had reported. Twelve characteristic properties common to 21 reported cases of deep dyslexia were listed by Coltheart (1980a). These properties were:

(1) semantic errors
(2) visual errors
(3) function-word substitutions
(4) derivational errors
(5) non-lexical derivation of phonology from print impossible
(6) lexical derivation of phonology from print impaired
(7) low-imageability words harder to read aloud than high-imageability words
(8) verbs are harder than adjectives, which are harder than nouns, in reading aloud
(9) function words harder than content words in reading aloud
(10) writing spontaneously, or to dictation, is impaired
(11) auditory–verbal short-term memory is impaired
(12) whether a word can be read aloud at all depends on its context.

Some properties listed here require comment. Properties 5 and 6 refer to the fact that neither nonwords (non-lexical stimuli) nor words (lexical stimuli) appear to be able to be pronounced aloud using direct mappings from orthography to phonology. Properties 10 and 11 refer to associated difficulties with writing and short-term memory, rather than to properties of reading *per se*. Unfortunately, little further work has been carried out on the relationship between these aspects of language processing and deep dyslexia.

Property 12 refers to the finding that when homographic words (i.e. words with identical spellings but different meanings) are presented in sentences for oral reading, success may depend upon the grammatical role played by the word in a sentence. Thus, a French-speaking deep dyslexic patient was able to read aloud the written word "car" in the sentence "Le *car* ralentit *car* le moteur chauffe" (the car slowed down because the motor overheated) only when it occupied the position of a noun in the sentence, as in "Le car". The subject was unable to read aloud "car" when it occupied the position of a conjunction as in "car le motor chauffe" (Andreewsky, Deloche, & Kossanyi, 1980). What the findings of Andreewsky et al. reveal is that deep dyslexic subjects who are sensitive to the grammatical role of words in sentences must be processing the syntax of the sentence in order for the grammatical role to affect oral reading. This potentially informative aspect of deep dyslexia has had little further investigation.

Subsequent studies have suggested that some properties listed by Coltheart (1980a) are not independent of each other and may be subsumed. In particular, the grammatical word-class effect in *single* word reading is now known to vary consistently with differences in the concreteness/imageability of the words.

CONCRETENESS, IMAGEABILITY, AND THE GRAMMATICAL WORD-CLASS EFFECT

Intuitively, concrete and abstract words seem to draw on meanings derived from different sorts of experience: concrete words generally refer to "objects, materials or persons" experienced in the physical world (Paivio, 1969; Spreen & Schulz, 1966), whereas abstract words are marked by an absence of such properties and instead relate to information obtained from verbal experiences in the mental world of thought and ideas. These differences appear to have psychological significance since concrete words are processed more readily than abstract words in a variety of tasks, including free recall; recognition memory; short-term memory; paired-associate learning; and oral reading (see Paivio, Yuille, & Madigan, 1968; Paivio, 1991). Paivio et al. (1968) argued that because concrete nouns are consistently associated with the physical world, they readily arouse sensory images that support processing in linguistic tasks. On the basis of this, they proposed that the psychological construct underlying the concreteness effects was imagery.

Paivio et al. (1968) collected ratings for imagery (based on the capacity of words to arouse a sensory experience such as a mental picture or sound) and correlated these with ratings for concreteness (based on their capacity to arouse sensory experiences of "objects, materials or persons"). They found that ratings for imageability and concreteness correlated very highly ($r = 0.83$). In general, words received equivalent ratings on each scale, with the exception of words relating to emotions, such as *agony*, and *love* (which produced higher ratings for imageability than concreteness), and a set of fairly unfamiliar object names (that received higher ratings for concreteness than imageability). Paivio et al. concluded that concreteness and imageability scales "appear to be defining a common dimension of word meaning derived from associations of the words with concrete objects and events". He suggested that "for research purposes either scale, or a combination of the two, can be used for item selection" (Paivio et al., 1968, p. 7).

The possibility that the grammatical word-class effect in deep dyslexia might be accounted for by differences in the imageability/concreteness of words in different grammatical classes was examined by Shallice and Warrington (1975), and rejected. They used a set of nouns, adjectives, and verbs matched for moderate levels of concreteness, but not for imageability.

There was a significant grammatical word-class effect, benefiting adjectives and showing the greatest disadvantage to verbs. The advantage for adjectives in set 2 was argued to arise from the inclusion of seven colour names in the set of adjectives, which KF read well (6/7 correct). This good performance with colour names probably reflects the failure to control for imageability: colour names are low in concreteness but are highly imageable words (Funnell, 1983).

Subsequent studies have provided more compelling evidence that word-class differences in deep dyslexic reading are confounded with imageability/concreteness. Barry and Richardson (1988) found that part-of-speech had no effect on GR's reading when concreteness and frequency were statistically controlled. Similarly, Allport and Funnell (1981) showed that the advantage to nouns compared to verbs, apparent in the reading of five deep dyslexic subjects (including PW and DE), disappeared once differences in imageability and word frequency had been controlled. Overall, these studies suggest that apparent grammatical word class effects in deep dyslexic reading are the result of a confound with intrinsic differences in the concreteness/imageability of the words in each class, rather than a genuine effect of differences in grammatical role.

CONCRETENESS/IMAGEABILITY AND READING ERRORS

Semantic errors

As noted earlier, semantic errors tend to occur to concrete rather than to abstract words. Barry (1984) analysed GR's reading responses (collected by Marshall and Newcombe) and found that GR made semantic errors to words that were less concrete than the words he could read correctly, but more concrete than the words he failed to attempt to read. Words with a mean concreteness value of 5.52 he read correctly; but he made semantic errors to words with a mean concreteness value of 4.55; and he failed to respond to words with a mean concreteness value of 4.16. These differences were significant. Earlier, Shallice and Warrington (1975) had noted that KF made semantic errors to words that were lower in imageability than the words he read correctly.

To explain the effect of imageability level upon the incidence of semantic errors, Newton and Barry (1997) proposed that highly concrete concepts are more likely to specify an exact lexical representation than less concrete words that are more likely to specify a range of semantically related lexical representations, or synonyms, a number of which may be sufficiently activated to become candidates for a response.

Visual errors

Visual errors, on the other hand, are more likely to be produced as responses to abstract words than to concrete words (Morton & Patterson, 1980b; Shallice & Warrington, 1975) and tend to be more concrete than the stimulus words that prompted the error (Shallice & Warrington, 1975).

Patterson (1978) suggested originally that the lexical orthographic codes for the words that produced visual errors might have been damaged, but revised this view when she found that PW and DE were able to recognise the orthographic patterns in lexical decision tasks of many words that they were unable either to read aloud or comprehend (Patterson, 1979).

A now widely accepted explanation of visual errors was put forward by Shallice and Warrington (1980), who proposed that the orthographic word-form system has the ability to activate the semantic representations of more than one word at once. If the meaning is unavailable for an abstract word, then an orthographically similar word with an imageable/concrete meaning, may be produced instead. A visually related error of higher concreteness would then be produced that is unrelated to the target word in meaning. This theory predicts that the abstract words to which deep dyslexic subjects fail to respond, should be those that lack visually similar neighbours with imageable/concrete meanings—a prediction that does not appear to have been investigated empirically.

Derivational errors

Derivational errors (e.g. beg→beggar), which are morphologically related (in this case by sharing the root morpheme "beg") are also both visually and semantically related to the target. These errors were originally referred to as "visual completion errors" by Marshall and Newcombe (1966) and as "derivational semantic errors" (i.e. semantic errors that share a root morpheme) by Shallice and Warrington (1975).

Initial studies by Moody (1984), of four patients who made morphologically related reading errors, suggested that derivational errors were truly morphological. Moody presented her subjects with *truly suffixed* words (such as *officer*) and *pseudo-suffixed* words (such as *corner*), which were matched for imageability and word frequency. She found that errors were much more likely to occur to suffixed, than to the pseudo-suffixed, words (i.e. errors of the type *officer*→"office" occurred more frequently than *corner*→"corn"). Job and Sartori (1984) reported a similar result using pre-fixed and pseudo-prefixed words matched for word frequency and word length, but not for differences in imageability/concreteness. The reading errors that appeared to specifically affect morphologically complex words were argued to support a morphological process in visual word recognition, in which root morphemes (such as "office") were processed separately from affixes (such as "er").

A further study by Funnell (1987) produced a different result. In this study both words and stems were matched as closely as possible for imageability/concreteness and word frequency. For example, affixed words, such as *buyer*, were matched to pseudo-affixed words, such as *wither*, for both the overall imageability of the word (e.g. *buyer* 4.63; *wither* 4.38) and stem (e.g. *buy* 3.97; *with* 3.87). With these controls for imageability across word sets, there was no significant difference in the ability of the deep dyslexic patient JG to orally read suffixed and pseudo-suffixed words.

Function word substitutions

Semantic and derivational errors can be explained by arguing that words that have access to some imageable/concrete elements of word meaning will produce semantic errors, whereas those that do not will either produce a visually related error with a more imageable but unrelated meaning, or no overt response. But the remaining type of error—function word substitutions—has not been thought to fit this pattern. For example, Shallice (1988) notes that function words receive very low ratings for imageability/concreteness and yet do not usually produce visually related words as errors; moreover, the errors are not usually more concrete.

This generally held view is not supported by an analysis carried out by Morton and Patterson (1980a) of the function word errors made by PW, from which they concluded that function words "are treated no differently from content words" by the semantic processes involved in written word identification. Morton and Patterson found that PW made both visual errors and semantic errors to function words, and that errors were frequently more concrete than the stimulus word. A post hoc analysis of the error responses made by PW and DE (listed in Coltheart, Patterson, & Marshall, 1980, 1987a, Appendix 2) supports this view. As Table 2.4 shows, visual and semantic errors occur to function words, many producing content word responses that are more concrete/imageable than the target.

Morton and Patterson (1980a) investigated PW's comprehension of function words and found considerable understanding of the semantic aspects of *gender* (e.g. he/she), *number* (e.g. few/many), *frequency* (e.g. few/all) and *spatial reference* (e.g. above/below). However, they did not relate the evidence for knowledge of function word meaning with the subjects' reading errors. When this comparison is made, (using PW's reading errors listed in Coltheart et al., 1980, 1987a, Appendix 2), a strong relationship between comprehension and reading errors is found. Of the target words that gave rise to semantic and visual-semantic errors, 97% could be classified into groups according to aspects of word meaning that PW was sensitive to: (1)

TABLE 2.4
A re-analysis of errors to function words made by PW and DE from data reported in
Coltheart et al. (1980, Appendix 2).

	PW	DE
Total number of errors	171	20
Error types:		
Unrelated responses	89	6
	to–we	was–and
	are–with	off–from
Visually related function words	23	5
	what–why	they–the
	ever–over	by–my
Visually related content words	21	2
	across–cross	what–hat
	do–doll	what–hat
Semantically related function words	22	1
	down–under	his–he
	his–we	
Semantically related content words	8	0
	he–man	
	if–query	
Visual/semantic related function words	6	6
	hers–she	your–you
	where–whither	have–has
Visual/semantic related content words	2	0
	down–downstairs	
	several–seven	

words that refer to *gender* (e.g. pronouns: *us*→"we"); (2) words that refer to *number* (e.g. *some*→"many"); (3) words that refer to *frequency or time* (e.g. *usually*→"sometimes"); and (4) words that refer to *position or direction in space* (e.g. *where*→"whither"). Only three errors failed to fit this grouping: *therefore*→"because", *if*→"query" (both made by PW), and *have*→"has" (made by DE).

Unusually in reports of cases of deep dyslexia, PW read a proportion of function words correctly: on average 23% across a selection of function word classes, including prepositions and conjunctions; adverbs and quantifiers; interrogatives; auxiliary verbs; and personal pronouns. Prepositions and conjunctions and auxiliary verbs presented in isolation have little referential meaning and it seems unlikely that these words were read aloud successfully on the basis of lexical semantic mappings between orthography and phonology. It is more likely that these words, which are among the most common words in the reading vocabulary, were read aloud by residual lexical phonological processes which map orthographic word forms directly onto phonological word forms and which are known to favour the reading of high frequency words (Funnell, 1987; Strain, Patterson, & Seidenberg, 1995).

EXPLAINING THE CONCRETENESS/
IMAGEABILITY EFFECT

It was reported earlier that imageable words were thought by Paivio (1969) to gain their advantage in many psychological tasks from the fact that these words could produce mental images. Adopting this view, Richardson (1975) suggested that the advantage for imageable words in deep dyslexia reflected the use of a strategy in which the subject forms a mental image of the object referred to by the written word which is then named. This proposal implies that words that cannot be imaged within this system will not be named. Barry and Richardson (1988) later rescinded this view, and others have also rejected the idea that a process of imagery is necessarily involved in deep dyslexic reading (Shallice, 1988; Shallice & Warrington, 1975). The fact that some words access semantic representations with imageable properties does not presuppose that access to the properties necessitates the use of imagery.

As Baddeley, Ellis, Miles, and Lewis (1982, p. 196) have argued, although imageability is a "potent variable" in readability, "it has virtually no explanatory power". In an attempt to provide explanatory power, Jones (1985) proposed that differences in imageability reflect differences in the ease with which words summon the semantic predicates on which reading responses are based. He asked subjects to rate written words for ease of predication (EoP) which he defined as the ease with which what words refer to "can be described by single factual statements". He gave as examples of predicates "A dog is an animal"; "A dog has four legs"; "A dog barks when it is angry", and so on. The mean EoP ratings obtained for a set of 100 words were found to correlate very highly (0.88) with imageability ratings obtained from Paivio's norms. On the basis of this association, Jones (1985, p. 7) argued that "the concept of ease of predication provides a principled account of ... the probability with which individual nouns are read correctly by deep dyslexics".

Further analyses revealed that ratings of EoP varied systematically with grammatical word class. When word classes were ordered according to EOP ratings, the order obtained (nouns→adjectives→verbs→function words) mirrored the order observed generally in cases of deep dyslexia (Jones, 1985). EoP ratings were also found to decrease systematically across the word sets which our classic deep dyslexic subject GR either read correctly; read as a semantic error; or failed to make a reading response to (Barry, 1984). Thus, the explanatory power of EoP appeared to receive independent support from these studies. However, differences in imageability are also known to vary with both grammatical class and oral reading performance, so it could be argued that these results merely reflect the close relationship between ratings of EoP and imageability. Although Jones assumes a causal role for EoP in deep dyslexia, this is based on correlations which cannot determine causality. As Breedin, Saffran, and Coslett (1994) point out, the alternative direction of causation is possible: i.e. that imageability facilitates predication.

Jones (1985) does not explain what EoP ratings actually measure. He mentions the possibility that EoP reflects variability in predicate distributions, but notes that little is known about this variable. Examples that he provides of attempts to investigate predicate distributions emphasise the commonality of features: either the number of features which members of categories share, or the features shared by words in similies (such as "Billboards are warts") in which basically unrelated items are compared. However, in the instructions given to the subjects about rating words for EoP, the number of statements that can be made about a word appears to be the critical variable. As de Mornay Davies (1997; de Mornay Davies & Funnell, in press) points out, Jones gives the word "dog" as an example of an imageable word and then provides no less than 11 examples of statements that could be made. In contrast, he suggests that the abstract word *idea* "would probably be judged as very difficult to make simple factual statements about" (Jones, 1985, p. 6), and gives no examples at all.

Actual examples of predicates and features for words were collected by de Mornay Davies (1997). He asked subjects to generate predicates and features for a set of 30 concrete and 30 abstract words (which included a subset of Jones's words: 10 words with high concreteness ratings and 10 with low). He defined predicates as "facts, beliefs or attitudes about or toward something" and gave as examples responses such "wheels", "vehicle", "ride them" for the target word "bicycle". As examples of *characteristic features* he provided "wheels", "pedals", "saddles", etc. (p. 304). He found that overall subjects produced significantly more predicates and features to concrete words compared to abstract words. Moreover, the number of predicates and the number of features obtained to the words from Jones (1985) correlated to a highly significant level with the EoP ratings that Jones provided: EoP/pred 0.85; EoP/feat 0.80.

However, when de Mornay Davies (1997) confined the correlations to either concrete or abstract words, EoP ratings did not correlate significantly with the number of predicates or features generated. This is surprising because, as Fig. 2.1 shows, the number of predicates and features varied quite widely within each set: the range of predicates for abstract and concrete words varied from 2.6 to 5.9 and 6.2 to 10.3 respectively; and ranges for features for abstract and concrete words varied from 2.3 to 6.4 and 5.1 to 9.6 respectively. In fact, the number of predicates and features for abstract and concrete words formed a continuum linking the two groups of words; yet differences in EoP ratings varied only slightly between words within the abstract and concrete word sets, and showed no regular increase with increasing numbers of predicates or features. Instead, ease of predica-

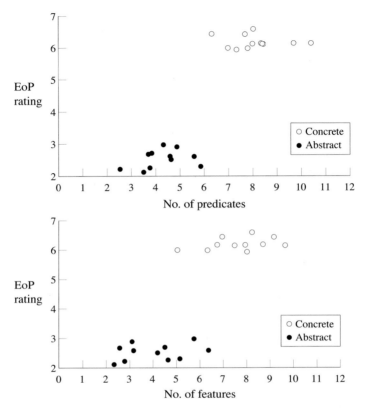

FIG. 2.1   Experiment 1: Ease of predication ratings for concrete and abstract words plotted against the number of predicates and features generated.

tion ratings split the continuum into dichotomous sets of words with high or low EoP ratings that perfectly honoured the distinction between levels of high and low imageability for which the words were originally selected. Correlations of EoP with concreteness (0.99) and imageability (0.87) were greater than correlations between EoP and predicates (0.85) and features (0.80) and, in the case of concreteness, significantly so.

In a second experiment, in which words were drawn from all levels on the abstract–concrete scale, the number of predicates and features generated for the two word sets overlapped considerably. Nevertheless, as Fig. 2.2 shows, EoP ratings continued to completely separate the two word groups. Thus, the number of predicates or features generated for words does not distinguish between words with high or low EoP ratings, nor with high or low ratings of imageability or concreteness. Differences in EoP simply seem to reflect differences in concreteness/imageability. In short, the basis for the claimed explanatory power of ease of predication has proved to be elusive.

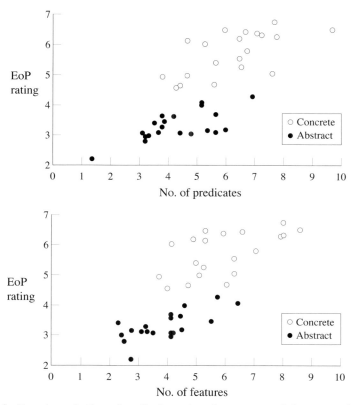

FIG. 2.2 Experiment 2: Ease of predication ratings for concrete and abstract words plotted against the number of predicates and features generated.

In particular, there appears to be no evidence to support the view that concreteness/imageability effects in deep dyslexia reflect differences in the number of predicates or features that represent the concepts. As we shall see, this finding raises problems for connectionist models of deep dyslexia, which are based upon such assumptions.

CONNECTIONIST MODELS OF DEEP DYSLEXIA

Connectionist models are working simulations of computational processes. The models are composed of a network of interconnected units that can learn about consistently occurring patterns available in the information to which it is exposed. They can be trained to an optimal level of performance and then "lesioned" by removing some connections or introducing noise. When such models are lesioned, the impaired performance of the model can be compared to the characteristic performance of brain-damaged subjects to show whether the underlying architecture of the model can explain patterns of both normal and abnormal behaviour.

Simulation of reading errors in deep dyslexia

Hinton and Shallice (1991) were the first to use a connectionist model to simulate the characteristic reading errors found in deep dyslexia—notably, semantic errors, visual errors, and visual-and-semantic errors (errors related visually and semantically to the target: e.g. *rat*→"cat"). Their model consisted of a network composed of two sets of representations: a set of grapheme units representing particular letters in particular positions in the word, and a set of semantic units. The grapheme units were connected to the semantic units by a set of intermediate units. The semantic feature units (referred to as semene units) represented the semantic features of words belonging to five different semantic categories: *indoor objects*, *animals*, *body parts*, *foods*, and *outdoor objects*. The semantic units were connected to each other by local connections between closely related semantic features, such as between different colours. A further set of semantic "clean up" units, received connections from some semantic units and sent connections to others, building higher-order semantic relationships based upon consistently occurring feature sets, in order to provide more global semantic descriptions. The model was trained to identify and activate the precise meaning for 40 short words drawn from the five semantic categories selected. The model was then "lesioned" (by removing some units or connections at random or by introducing noise into the system) and was found to produce errors characteristic of deep dyslexia at levels above those expected by chance. All lesion sites produced semantic, visual, and visual/semantic errors, although visual errors were more likely to occur with damage closer to the grapheme units and semantic errors were more likely to occur with damage closer to the semantic units.

Simulations of concrete-abstractness effects

Plaut and Shallice (1993) extended Hinton and Shallice's connectionist modelling of deep dyslexia in order to investigate the concreteness effect. They took 20 pairs of four-letter words, each pair containing one concrete and one abstract word that were closely visually similar, differing by only one letter: for example *tart–tact*; *hare–hire*. Taking differences in EoP as a guide, they assigned twice as many semantic features to concrete words than to abstract words. In total there were 98 semantic features: 67 represented features of concrete words (for example "has legs", "is soft", "found in woods"), and 31

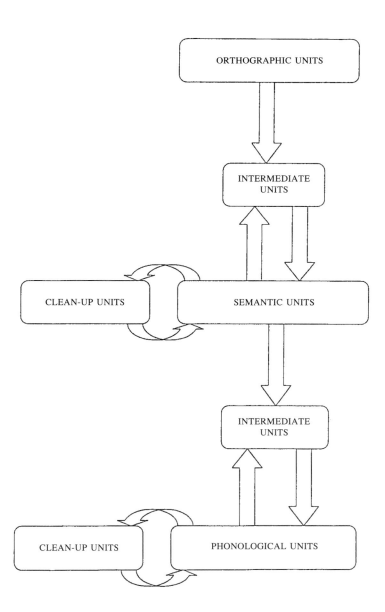

FIG. 2.3 A connectionist network for mapping orthography to phonology via semantics (redrawn from Plaut & Shallice, 1993).

features (such as "has duration", "relates to power", "temporary"), represented abstract words. The assignment of these sets of semantic representations separated the semantic representations of concrete and abstract words virtually completely. Just a few concrete words mapped onto some abstract features, but no abstract words mapped onto concrete features. Thus, the meanings of concrete and abstract words were distinguished by both the number and the nature of the semantic features assigned.[3]

The design of the model is shown in Fig. 2.3. The orthographic units were connected to a set of semantic units via a set of intermediate units. These connections from orthography to semantics are referred to by Plaut and Shallice as the *"direct pathway"*. The semantic units also connected back to the (orthographic) intermediate units. The semantic units were not interconnected, but were linked to clean-up units which established higher order (superordinate) units from features that were consistently activated together. This part of the model was referred to by Plaut and Shallice as the *"clean-up pathway"*. The semantic units also connected to a set of phonological units via a set of intermediate units.

Once the model had been trained to produce the correct phonological and semantic outputs to each orthographic input, it was lesioned at different locations and the phonological output recorded. Overall, concrete words were processed more successfully than abstract words, in line with the characteristic pattern observed in deep dyslexia, but this effect was confined to lesions to the *direct pathway* that linked orthography to semantics. Even mild lesions to this pathway (removing 5% of the connections) produced a marked advantage for concrete words. Lesions to this pathway also produced errors that tended to be more concrete than the target word. Semantic errors and visual errors, in which the target and response overlapped by two or more letters, were found with lesions to all locations. Abstract words were particularly likely to produce visual errors which were more concrete. Plaut and Shallice concluded that when the direct route was lesioned, the network simulated deep dyslexia by showing first, overall better performance for concrete than abstract words; second, a tendency for errors to be more concrete than the stimuli; and third, a higher proportion of visual errors to abstract words.

---

[3] Plaut and Shallice do not explain the principles upon which they decided to assign twice as many features to concrete words than to abstract words. Although ease-of-predication ratings indicated a difference in the proportion of features associated with concrete and abstract words, the proportion of 2:1 appears to be an arbitrary figure. In addition, no motivation was provided for selecting mostly non-overlapping features to represent concrete and abstract words. In fact, the meanings of many abstract words and concrete words appear to be closely associated: for example, the concept for the word "education", besides entailing concepts underlying further abstract words such as learning and teaching, entails concrete concepts, such as school, children, teachers, blackboards, and so on. Likewise, concrete words such as "school", entail the concept "education".

It is worth noting that the characteristics of the stimulus set are responsible for the findings. As reported earlier, visually similar pairs of concrete and abstract words were selected that differed by only one letter (e.g. *tent–rent*; *tart–tact*; *face–fact*). When orthographic similarity is computed across all possible concrete–abstract word pairings in the word set, 92% of the words that differ by one letter from the concrete words were found to be abstract words; likewise, 92% of the words that differ by one letter from abstract words were found to be concrete words. This relationship between visual similarity and the concreteness–abstractness pairings predicts that when visual errors occurred, the responses were virtually certain to belong to the opposing semantic set; that is, visual errors to abstract words were most likely to be concrete words, and visual errors to concrete words were most likely to be abstract words. This close link between orthographic similarity and opposing semantic category is most *un*likely to represent the normal relationship between orthographic similarity and dimensions of concreteness/abstractness in the vocabulary of human beings.

In contrast to the concreteness effects that emerged from even mild lesions to the direct pathway, neither mild nor moderate lesions to the clean-up pathways (connecting the semantic units with the clean-up units bi-directionally) had differing effects on concrete and abstract words. Severe lesions, on the other hand, had a surprising differential effect upon performance: sparing the reading of abstract words relative to concrete words and producing errors to concrete words that tended to be more abstract than the target. Thus, severe lesions to the clean-up units produced the reverse effect to that observed in deep dyslexia.

To explain the appearance of the reverse concreteness effect, Plaut and Shallice argued that the model's representation of the meaning of concrete words and abstract words depended upon different pathways. Concrete word meanings were particularly dependent upon the clean-up units, which were strongly engaged in connecting together the numerous semantic features, belonging to concrete words. In contrast, abstract words possessed fewer semantic features: they were less effective at engaging the clean-up units and more dependent upon representations of meaning in the direct pathway. Thus, when the clean-up units were severely damaged, with detrimental consequences for the meaning of concrete words, the meaning of abstract words was relatively unaffected.

As Plaut and Shallice pointed out, a reverse concreteness effect has been observed in a subject (CAV) reported by Warrington (1981). This patient read abstract words more successfully than concrete words, and also produced visually similar abstract words as errors to concrete words, thus providing psychological plausibility for the model's poor performance to concrete words following severe lesions to the clean-up units. The fact that CAV did not, in fact, make semantic errors in reading—a pattern that would be predicted by the model—was explained by the fact that CAV had some phonic abilities and that this would perhaps have acted to screen out semantic errors.

The analogy between the model's performance when the clean-up units were damaged and CAV's abilities does not stretch far, however. The reverse concreteness effect demonstrated by the model appeared with severe lesions to the semantic representations of concrete words in the system. By analogy, CAV should have had very severely impaired comprehension for concrete words. Tests show, however, that CAV's vocabulary score on the WAIS was slightly above average (11) and that his ability to match concrete words to pictures was not particularly impaired relative to abstract words (21/30 and 25/30 correct respectively). Thus, although the model has demonstrated a reverse concreteness effect in oral reading, and one that fits the characteristics of CAV's oral reading, the model predicts severe comprehension problems that are not found in CAV's performance.

Plaut and Shallice point out that the concreteness effect has emerged from a system that processes the meanings of both concrete and abstract words within a network in which the differing numbers of semantic features have differing influence on the development of the attractors which the model builds during learning. However, the plausibility of this manipulation for normal processing is under question. It was reported earlier that counts of numbers of features produced by subjects to concrete and abstract words failed to distinguish clearly between concrete and abstract words when these were selected across the full range of concreteness (de Mornay Davies, 1997). Thus, the critical assumption upon which the semantic processing of the model is based does not appear to be supported by the data.

THE RIGHT HEMISPHERE HYPOTHESIS FOR DEEP DYSLEXIA

The theoretical question that has driven the direction of research into deep dyslexia over the past decade was posed by Coltheart (1980b). How is it, he asked, that when a subject makes semantic errors all other characteristics of deep dyslexia, such as the inability to read function words, the abolishment of the ability to read nonwords, and the presence of visual errors, also occur. In an attempt to explain the pattern of errors found in deep dyslexia within a functional model of normal reading, Morton and Patterson (1980b) proposed four separate lesions to explain the effects of abstractness, derivational errors, failure to read nonwords, and semantic errors. However, as Coltheart, Patterson, and Marshall (1987b) point out, separable lesions suggest that, in principle, each lesion should be expected also to occur independently, so that sometimes semantic errors should occur without the other characteristics. The fact that they do not raises problems for this explanation.

Since the co-occurring pattern of characteristic features of deep dyslexia did not appear to be accounted for readily within a model of normal reading, an alternative hypothesis was put forward (Coltheart, 1980b; Marcel & Patterson, 1978; Saffran, Bogyo, Schwartz, & Marin, 1980). This suggested that the characteristics of deep dyslexia were arising from right hemisphere processing, a part of the brain generally thought not to be involved in normal reading. This theory was supported by widespread damage to the language areas of the left hemisphere processes revealed in the CT scans of five deep dyslexic patients (Coltheart et al., 1980, Appendix 1). Such large lesions suggested that it was unlikely that oral reading in deep dyslexia could be carried out by left hemisphere processes (Coltheart, 1980b).

At the time that the right hemisphere hypothesis was first proposed, independent support for semantic processing of concrete words in the right hemisphere was available from two sources: (1) hemi-field studies using intact subjects, and (2) studies of right hemisphere language using split-brain patients. As Coltheart (1980b) reported, hemi-field studies at that time generally revealed a processing advantage for written abstract words in the left hemisphere compared to the right hemisphere, with no difference across hemispheres for concrete words. Studies of split-brain subjects, in which the corpus callosum had been sectioned (separating the cortical connections between the cerebral hemispheres), also showed an advantage for concrete words compared to abstract words when the words were presented to the right hemisphere.

Subsequent reviews questioned the reliability of the evidence for the concreteness effect using these hemi-field and split-brain techniques (Coltheart et al., 1987b; Patterson & Besner, 1984). As a further challenge to the right hemisphere hypothesis, Patterson and Besner (1984) proposed that deep dyslexia reflected the use of both left and right hemisphere processes. They came to this conclusion after reviewing the reading performance of two patients, reported by Zaidel (1982), whose left hemisphere had been surgically removed. Both subjects demonstrated characteristics of deep dyslexic reading but appeared to be poorer readers than two deep dyslexic subjects (PW and DE) with whom they were compared. To explain this effect, Patterson and Besner proposed that deep dyslexic subjects may have access to additional resources for reading beyond right hemisphere processes. A more recent study also entertained the same conclusion (Patterson, Vargha-Khadem, & Polkey, 1989); although other reasons, such as the effect of early hemispherectomy on the development of reading, and the consequences of possible damage to right hemisphere processes from seizures, were considered too.

Recently, attempts have been made to investigate the right hemisphere hypothesis of deep dyslexia using functional imaging techniques. A study by Weekes, Coltheart, and Gordon (1997) found evidence for the involvement of right hemisphere processes in the visual recognition of written words in a subject with deep dyslexia. However, in this condition, the stimulus words were confined to function words, so that no definite conclusion can be drawn from this experiment concerning the right hemisphere's involvement in the recognition of concrete words. A further experiment, which used concrete words, demonstrated superior processing of spoken output processes in the left hemisphere, but regrettably, semantic processes—critical to the right hemisphere hypothesis of reading—were not investigated.

An earlier brain-imaging study of two deep dyslexia subjects, conducted by Price, Howard et al. (1998), found that increases in cerebral blood flow during the oral reading of concrete words occurred primarily in structures lying *outside* the sylvian areas of the left temporal lobe. Both subjects showed greater activity in the *left* anterior temporal lobe compared to control subjects. Controls showed little activation in this area; instead, their patterns of activation during oral reading were restricted to the classic language areas of the left perisylvian fissure. Significantly, a previous study by Price, Moore, Humphreys, and Wise (1997) had identified areas activated in the left anterior temporal lobe during deep dyslexic reading as being implicated in semantic processing.

Price, Howard et al. (1998) concluded from their study that the patterns of increased activation in deep dyslexic reading occur mainly in spared regions of the *left* hemisphere, but they recognised that there was also evidence for increased activity in some areas of the right hemisphere. They found that both deep dyslexic subjects showed greater activity in the *right* inferior occipital gyrus and in the *right* parahippocampal gyrus: areas that are thought to be involved in processing visual objects rather than written words. Thus, current evidence from both left hemispherectomy and brain-imaging studies appears to favour an account of deep dyslexia in terms of the recruitment of both left and right hemisphere processes.

SINGLE-WORD NAMING AND NOMINAL REFERENCE

As Marshall and Newcombe (1966) pointed out, in the original study of GR, the oral reading of *isolated* written words is a "highly unnatural" task. Reading tasks normally require the extraction of information from text. In such tasks, the semantic and syntactic context of words contribute to building connections between propositions, often requiring only the gist (or sense) of word meaning to be retrieved. The natural role for single words is to act as *names* for things. Perhaps, then, the natural process to apply to the unnatural task of single word naming is to treat the stimulus word as part of an elementary syntactic frame denoting "it", in which the function words denoting reference (such as "the", "a", "an") have been omitted.

Martinus Nijhoff Publishers.

Barry, C., & Richardson, J.T.E. (1988). Accounts of oral reading in deep dyslexia. In H.A. Whitaker (Ed.), *Phonological processes and brain mechanisms* (pp. 119–171). New York: Springer-Verlag.

Breedin, S.D., Saffran, E.M., & Coslett, H.B. (1994). Reversal of the concreteness effect in a patient with semantic dementia. *Cognitive Neuropsychology, 11*, 617–660.

Chomsky, N. (1965). *Aspects of the theory of syntax*. Cambridge, MA: MIT Press.

Coltheart, M. (1980a). Deep dyslexia: A review of the syndrome. In M. Coltheart, K. Patterson, & J.C. Marshall (Eds), *Deep dyslexia* (pp. 22–47). London: Routledge & Kegan Paul.

Coltheart, M. (1980b). Deep dyslexia: A right-hemisphere hypothesis. In M. Coltheart, K. Patterson, & J.C. Marshall (Eds), *Deep dyslexia* (pp. 326–380). London: Routledge & Kegan Paul.

Coltheart, M., Curtis, B., Atkins, P., & Haller, M. (1993). Models of reading aloud: Dual-route and parallel-distributed-processing approaches. *Psychological Review, 100*, 589–608.

Coltheart, M., Patterson, K., & Marshall, J.C. (1980). *Deep dyslexia*. London: Routledge & Kegan Paul.

Coltheart, M., Patterson, K., & Marshall, J.C. (1987a). *Deep dyslexia* (2nd ed.). London: Routledge & Kegan Paul.

Coltheart, M., Patterson, K., & Marshall, J.C. (1987b). Deep dyslexia since 1980. In M. Coltheart, K. Patterson, & J.C. Marshall (Eds), *Deep dyslexia* (2nd ed., pp. 407–451). London: Routledge & Kegan Paul.

De Mornay Davies, P. (1997). *The semantic representation of concrete and abstract words*. Uupublished, PhD thesis, Royal Holloway University of London, UK.

De Mornay Davies, P., & Funnell, E. (in press). Semantic representation and ease of predication. *Brain and Language*.

Funnell, E. (1983). *Ideographic communication in aphasia*. Unpublished PhD thesis, University of Reading, UK.

Funnell, E. (1987). Morphological errors in acquired dyslexia: A case of mistaken identity. *Quarterly Journal of Experimental Psychology, 39A*, 497–539.

Funnell, E., & Allport, D.A. (1987). Non-linguistic cognition and word meanings: Neuropsychological exploration of common mechanisms. In A. Allport, D. MacKay, W. Prinz, & E. Scheerer (Eds), *Language perception and production: Relationships between listening, speaking, reading and writing* (pp. 367–403). London: Academic Press.

Goldstein, K. (1948). *Language and language disturbances*. New York: Grune & Stratton.

Hinton, G., & Shallice, T. (1991). Lesioning an attractor network: Investigations of acquired dyslexia. *Psychological Review, 98*, 74–95.

James, C.T. (1975). The role of semantic information in lexical decisions. *Journal of Experimental Psychology: Human Perception and Performance, 104*, 130–136.

Job, R., & Sartori, G. (1984). Morphological decomposition: Evidence from crossed phonological dyslexia. *Quarterly Journal of Experimental Psychology, 36A*, 435–458.

Jones, G.V. (1985). Deep dyslexia, imageability and ease of prediction. *Brain and Language, 24*, 1–19.

Katz, J.J., & Fodor, J.A. (1963). The structure of a semantic theory. *Language, 39*, 170–210.

Low, A.A. (1931). A case of agrammatism in the English language. *Archives of Neurology and Psychiatry, 25*, 555–597.

Marcel, A., & Patterson, K.E. (1978). Word recognition and production: Reciprocity in clinical and normal studies. In J. Requin (Ed.), *Attention and performance VII* (pp. 209–225). Hillsdale, NJ: Lawrence Erlbaum Associates Inc.

Marshall, J.C., & Newcombe, F. (1966). Syntactic and semantic errors in paralexia. *Neuropsychologia, 4*, 169–176.

Marshall, J.C., & Newcombe, F. (1973). Patterns of paralexia. *Journal of Psycholinguistic Research*, *2*, 175–199.

Moody, S. (1984). *Agrammatic reading in phonological dyslexia*. Unpublished PhD thesis, Birkbeck College, University of London, UK.

Morton, J., & Patterson, K.E. (1980a). "Little words—No!" In M. Coltheart, K. Patterson, & J.C. Marshall (Eds), *Deep dyslexia* (pp. 270–285). London: Routledge & Kegan Paul.

Morton, J., & Patterson, K.E. (1980b). A new attempt at an interpretation, or, an attempt at a new interpretation. In M. Coltheart, K. Patterson, & J.C. Marshall (Eds), *Deep dyslexia* (pp. 91–118). London: Routledge & Kegan Paul.

Newton, P.K., & Barry, C. (1997). Concreteness in word production but not word comprehension in deep dyslexia. *Cognitive Neuropsychology*, *14*, 481–510.

Paivio, A. (1969). Mental imagery in associative learning and memory. *Psychological Review*, *76*, 241–263.

Paivio, A. (1991). Dual coding theory: Retrospective and current status. *Canadian Journal of Psychology*, *45*, 255–287.

Paivio, A., Yuille, J.C., & Madigan, S.A. (1968). Concreteness, imagery, and meaningfulness values for 925 nouns. *Journal of Experimental Psychology*, *76*, 1–25.

Patterson, K.E. (1978). Phonemic dyslexia. Errors of meaning and the meaning of errors. *Quarterly Journal of Experimental Psychology*, *30*, 587–601.

Patterson, K.E. (1979). What is right with deep dyslexic patients? *Brain and Language*, *87*, 111–129.

Patterson, K.E., & Besner, D. (1984). Is the right hemisphere literate? *Cognitive Neuropsychology*, *1*, 315–342.

Patterson, K.E., & Marcel, A.J. (1977). Aphasia, dyslexia and phonological coding of written words. *Quarterly Journal of Experimental Psychology*, *29*, 307–318.

Patterson, K., Vargha-Khadem, F., & Polkey, C.E. (1989). Reading with one hemisphere. *Brain*, *112*, 39–63.

Plaut, D.C., & Shallice, T. (1993). Deep dyslexia: A case study of connectionist neuropsychology. *Cognitive Neuropsychology*, *10*, 377–500.

Price, C.J., Howard, D., Patterson, K., Warburton, E.A., Friston, K.J., & Frackowaik, R.S.J. (1998). A functional neuroimaging description of two deep dyslexic patients. *Journal of Cognitive Neuroscience*, *10*, 303–315.

Price, C.J., Moore, C.J., Humphreys, G.W., & Wise, R. (1997). Segregating semantic from phonological processes during reading. *Journal of Cognitive Neuroscience*, *9*, 727–733.

Richardson, J.T.E. (1995). The effect of word imageability in acquired dyslexia. *Neuropsychologia*, *113*, 281–288.

Saffran, E.M., Bogyo, L.C., Schwartz, M.F., & Marin, O.S.M. (1980). Does deep dyslexia reflect right-hemisphere reading? In M. Coltheart, K. Patterson, & J.C. Marshall (Eds), *Deep dyslexia* (pp. 381–406). London: Routledge & Kegan Paul.

Saffran, E.M., & Marin, O.S.M. (1977). Reading without phonology: Evidence from aphasia. *Quarterly Journal of Experimental Psychology*, *29*, 515–525.

Saffran, E.M., & Schwartz, M.F. (1994). Of cabbages and things: Semantic memory from a neuropsychological perspective—a tutorial review. In C. Umilta & M. Moscovitch (Eds), *Attention and performance XV* (pp. 507–536). Cambridge, MA: MIT Books.

Seidenberg, M., & McClelland, J.L. (1989). A distributed, developmental model of word recognition and naming. *Psychological Review*, *96*, 523–568.

Shallice, T. (1988). *From neuropsychology to mental structure*. Cambridge, UK: Cambridge University Press.

Shallice, T., & Warrington, E.K. (1975). Word recognition in a phonemic dyslexic patient. *Quarterley Journal of Experimental Psychology*, *27*, 187–199.

Shallice, T., & Warrington, E.K. (1980). Single and multiple component central dyslexic syndromes. In M. Coltheart, K. Patterson, & J.C. Marshall (Eds), *Deep dyslexia* (pp. 119–145). London: Routledge & Kegan Paul.

Silverberg, N., Vigliocco, G., Insalaco, D., & Garrett, M. (1998). When reading a sentence is easier than reading a "little" word: The role of production processes in deep dyslexics' reading aloud. *Aphasiology, 12,* 335–356.

Spreen, O., & Schulz, R.W. (1966). Parameters of abstraction, meaningfulness, and pronunciability for 329 nouns. *Journal of Verbal Learning and Verbal Behaviour, 5,* 459–468.

Strain, E., Patterson, K.E., & Seidenberg, M.S. (1995). Semantic effects in single-word naming. *Journal of Experimental Psychology: Learning, Memory and Cognition, 21,* 1140–1154.

Warrington, E.K. (1981). Concrete word dyslexia. *British Journal of Psychology, 72,* 175–196.

Weekes, B., Coltheart, M., & Gordon, E. (1997). Deep dyslexia and right hemisphere reading—a regional cerebral blood flow study. *Aphasiology, 11,* 1139–1158.

Zaidel, E. (1982). Reading by the disconnected right hemisphere: An aphasiological perspective. In Y. Zotterman (Ed.), *Dyslexia: Neuronal, cognitive and linguistic aspects* (pp. 67–91). Oxford, UK: Pergamon Press.

CHAPTER THREE

Phonological alexia: The case of the singing detective

Karalyn Patterson
MRC Cognition and Brain Sciences Unit, Cambridge, UK

INTRODUCTION

Reading is a complex form of human cognitive activity, but—in the form in which it is often studied by experimental cognitive psychologists and neuro-psychologists, namely the recognition, pronunciation, and comprehension of single written words—it is not so complex as to be impenetrable. A limited number of processing domains contribute to successful word reading, and thus, from the point of view of neuropsychological studies of reading, the underlying deficits that are responsible for the observed patterns of impaired reading behaviour are probably also limited in number. There may be subtle interactions between brain regions or cognitive processes that, when more thoroughly understood, will complicate the picture. Furthermore, in any complex skill (especially ones like reading that require explicit instruction), strategic factors may introduce considerable individual differences into both the normal processes and an individual's adaptation to their disruption by brain damage. Nonetheless, to judge by the popularity of normal and dis-ordered reading as a topic for research, it seems that cognitive psychologists and neuropsychologists consider an account of reading processes to be a tractable problem.

Apart from their relatively limited number, what other general assump-tions might we be able to make about the basic processes of reading? Given the evolutionarily recent advent of reading as a human skill, the brain struc-tures responsible for reading behaviour undoubtedly evolved for other purposes. This fact has led some investigators (e.g. Farah, Stowe, & Levinson, 1996; Strain, Patterson, Graham, & Hodges, 1996) to argue that any pattern of reading disorder should in principle be associated with, and explicable with reference to, a deficit in some more evolutionarily estab-lished domain of processing. Thus, for example, pure alexia, in which letter recognition is at best slowed and at worst frankly impaired, has been linked to a basic ability for rapid discrimination and identification of visual forms

(Behrmann, Plaut, & Nelson, 1998; Farah & Wallace, 1991; Friedman & Alexander, 1984; Sekuler & Behrmann, 1996). Reading may be especially vulnerable to even a mild disruption of this capacity, because letters are highly confusable visual forms and correct word recognition requires accurate identification of every letter in every position (or else English readers would always be confusing words like *altitude*, *attitude,* and *aptitude*). Therefore, although there have been pure alexic patients without any reported abnormality in general visual processing, the argument is that these cases were not assessed on non-reading tasks that make comparable demands on rapid identification of confusable shapes such as letters. Recent studies of pure alexic patients (mentioned earlier) that have probed more carefully for deficits in appropriate non-reading visual tasks have indeed observed them.

What about the pattern of impaired reading that is the topic of this chapter, phonological alexia? The key feature of this disorder is a marked lexicality advantage in reading aloud: The patients read real words well (though not necessarily to a *fully* normal level of accuracy or speed) but are significantly and sometimes profoundly impaired at generating appropriate pronunciations of novel letter strings (nonwords), even if these are simple, word-like, and short (e.g. *dake* or *gam*). This sounds like a deficit highly specific to learned processes of reading, and indeed it has been interpreted as such in most accounts of phonological alexia (e.g. Beauvois & Derouesné, 1979; Coltheart, 1985; Funnell, 1983; Patterson, 1982; Shallice & Warrington, 1980). In one of the very first articles on this topic, however, Derouesné & Beauvois (1979) proposed that phonological alexia might result from disruption to either of two different underlying abilities— graphemic parsing, or blending of phonological elements into a co-ordinated pronunciation; and although both of these were discussed as components of the procedure for nonword reading, the second is an ability that would support aspects of language ability other than reading. If this were the cause of phonological alexia, then any patient severely impaired at reading nonwords should also be poor at non-reading tasks which stress phonological skills. Examples of such tasks are concatenating a series of spoken elements into a co-ordinated pronunciation, especially an unfamiliar one (e.g. blend /də, eɪ, kə/ into "dake"), or perhaps just repeating long nonwords presented in already assembled form (e.g. repeat "presillimate"). We will return in a moment to Derouesné & Beauvois' (1979) other proposed form of phonological alexia, and to a more recent hypothesis by Friedman (1995) regarding two different underlying deficits; but first, what is the current status of the hypothesis that the deficit in phonological alexia is clearly phonological but not (that is, not selectively) alexic?

Setting aside those cases who were not tested on sufficiently demanding phonological tasks to permit a conclusion, a startlingly high proportion of phonological alexic patients do seem to have deficits in non-reading phonological tasks such as segmentation, blending, or repetition of nonwords. In a recent journal special issue on the topic of phonological alexia (*Cognitive Neuropsychology*, 1996, *13*, 6, edited by Coltheart), six different papers presented data from a total of 17 patients with the reading performance characteristic of phonological alexia; and every one of the 17 had an associated phonological deficit. Furthermore, there is at least an indication—somewhat hard to pin down given the variety of ways in which phonological abilities were tested and the variety of stimulus materials used to assess nonword reading across the different studies—that the severity of an individual's nonword reading impairment correlates with the degree of deficit in phonological manipulation tasks. For example, when Berndt, Haendiges, Mitchum, & Wayland (1996) asked their patients to read nonwords with high-probability grapheme–phoneme correspondences (GPCs), three of the 11 patients managed reasonably good performance (between 70 and 85% correct; this is probably still abnormal, though nonword reading is a skill whose level varies widely in the population of neurologically normal readers: see Masterson, 1985). All 11 cases were impaired on the phoneme blending task administered by Berndt et al.; but of the four highest scores obtained on blending, three of the four belonged to the same three patients with fair nonword reading success.

Shallice (1988) asserted that, of all the phonological alexic patients reported in the literature to that date who had been tested on non-reading phonological tasks, only one had achieved good performance: LB, studied by Derouesné & Beauvois (1985). In 1988, when this was probably one of a single-figure total, the importance of the association was perhaps debatable; but by 1996, when the number of well-documented cases was at least into double (though not triple) figures, it appears that only one additional exception has been reported (case RR: Bisiacchi, Cipolotti, & Denes, 1989). This observation provokes the following two comments.

First of all, many neuropsychologists take the view that the theoretical importance of a particular dissociation is as convincingly established by $N = 1$ or 2 as it would be if the dissociation were commonplace. They furthermore hold that common associations—which might arise from damage to more than one neuroanatomically adjacent region—have no theoretical importance. Although this is one major position with regard to dissociations, it is not the only possible view: "This is not to say that all instances of isolated strong dissociations are theoretically useless. This is to say, however, that they must be approached with a degree of wariness, pending the demonstration of their high prevalence ... [and they] should not be treated with an unrestrained enthusiasm as the major tool of neuropsychological discovery and theory-building" (Goldberg, 1995, p. 195). In other words, before concluding that phonological alexia can be interpreted as a specific reading impairment, we might like to see more than one or two documented cases without an accompanying non-reading phonological deficit.

Second, if the view that $N = 1$ or 2 is sufficient were to be accepted, we might require those one or two cases to represent a strong dissociation. According to Shallice (1988, pp. 227–228), in a strong, or classical, dissociation, the preserved ability yields performance preferably at the pre-morbid level and at least within the normal range, whilst the impaired ability is well outside the normal range. To interpret phonological alexia as a deficit specific to reading, one might demand a case with a classical dissociation between general phonological skills and nonword reading; but to interpret it as phonological alexia at all, one might ask for a classical dissociation between word and nonword reading. Was this true of LB and RR, the two cases in the literature thus far without a phonological deficit of much consequence?[1]

LB's word reading was not normal (function words: 82% correct; inflected verbs: 74% correct); and one might question whether his nonword reading was much outside the normal (wide) range (2-letter nonwords: 85% correct; 4–5 letter nonwords: 48%). RR was tested on a rather small number ($N = 10$–15) of items per word class, but scored at or very near perfect levels on both function words and inflected verbs, with a less-than-perfect score (83% correct) only on a set of lower-frequency abstract nouns. Once again, however, the word–nonword discrepancy was rather slight: RR correctly read 93% of CV, VC, and CCV nonsense syllables; and although her reported performance on nonwords (63% correct) was outside the range of the control subjects tested by Bisiacchi et al., this was the average score on a list including complex multisyllabic nonwords up to 10 letters in length (e.g. *aiulla*, *carpagna*). The authors did not indicate whether RR's nonword performance was significantly modulated by word length (either in letters or syllables/phonemes), but one might extrapolate from her near-perfect performance on 2–3 letter nonsense syllables to guess at a score for 4–5 letter nonwords of at least 70%. More seriously impaired phonological alexic patients, like some of those studied by Berndt et al. (1996) or Patterson and Marcel (1992), have had scores of 0–20% for 4–5 letter nonwords.

Now, as noted earlier, there have been at least two proposals in the

---

[1] The qualification "of much consequence" is added because both sets of investigators in fact concluded that the patient *had* some form of deficit in an aspect of phonological processing. In the case of LB (Derouesné & Beauvois, 1985), despite his success on phonological blending tasks without an orthographic stimulus, this was described as a "difficulty to build the whole phonological form" of a nonword. Bisiacchi et al. (1989) gave more prominence to RR's success in phonological manipulation tasks, and interpreted his deficit as one of phonological short-term memory. The function of this phonological buffer, however, was described as "holding segmented phonological information, in order to build a composite sound blend" (p. 315), which does not sound a million miles away from Derouesné and Beauvois' interpretation.

literature that two different underlying deficits might both yield phonological alexia, and that additional detailed tests are required to discriminate between the two variants. In both proposals, one variant is the account that we have been considering in the last few paragraphs, that a nonword reading deficit is just one reflection of a weak phonological system that produces words more successfully than nonwords because words are well-learned phonological patterns. In the original proposal by Derouesné and Beauvois (1979), the alternative version of phonological alexia was attributed to an impairment in the first stage of the grapheme–phoneme translation process: graphemic parsing. The idea here is that, in order to translate the component graphemes of a letter string into their corresponding phonemes, the reader must determine what these graphemes are. In languages such as English and French, this will not always be obvious: for example, the adjacent letters EA correspond to one phoneme in the word *reach* but two phonemes in the word *react*.

Derouesné and Beauvois (1979) argued that patients with a deficit of graphemic parsing should be more successful at reading nonwords in which every letter was a single grapheme (e.g. *iko*) than nonwords requiring the knowledge that two adjacent letters correspond to a single phoneme (e.g. *cau*) (these are French examples but in fact work for English, too). By contrast, they hypothesised that patients poor at nonword reading owing to a phonological deficit should be unaffected by this graphemic manipulation; instead, the nonword reading success of the phonological variant of patient should be sensitive to whether an orthographic nonword is a "pseudohomophone" (e.g. in English, *brane* vs. *brate*): the pronunciation of the former—even though associated in reading with a different spelling pattern (*brain*)—is well learned and so should be less demanding on the phonological assembly stage of non-lexical reading. In support of these hypotheses, Derouesné and Beauvois demonstrated that the nonword reading performance of two phonological alexic patients was facilitated by single-letter grapheme stimuli and unaffected by the phonological manipulation, whereas the performance of two others improved on pseudohomophones but showed no impact of the graphemic manipulation.

The four patients just described were reported to be essentially perfect at reading real words; but this assessment was based on a test in which all words were high-frequency concrete nouns. It is now well known that, for patients with a more severe acquired reading disorder resembling phonological dyslexia in some respects (deep dyslexia: Coltheart, Patterson, & Marshall, 1980; Marshall & Newcombe, 1973), concrete nouns yield by far the best success on tests of reading aloud, significantly better than either high-frequency abstract nouns or function words. Deep dyslexia is generally assumed to reflect complete loss of the ability to obtain the pronunciation of a written word except by first activating its meaning, with the consequence that the patients fail utterly to read any nonwords correctly and have an advantage for words with rich, well-definable semantic representations, i.e. concrete nouns. This leads us to the second, and more recent, proposal of two different forms of phonological dyslexia.

Friedman's (1995) proposal starts from a position that rejects the classical dual-route assumption that readers need two separate procedures for translating orthography to phonology without reference to meaning: a lexical route that can directly activate pronunciations for all familiar words, and a separate non-lexical procedure that translates any letter string into a rule-governed pronunciation (Coltheart, 1985; Coltheart, Curtis, Atkins, & Haller, 1993). In Friedman's view of the reading process (similar to the "triangle" model of Plaut, McClelland, Seidenberg, & Patterson, 1996 and Seidenberg & McClelland, 1989), there is a single network for direct orthography-to-phonology (O→P) activation which handles both words and nonwords, plus a semantic reading route (O→S→P). Friedman then goes on to argue that, in addition to the variant of phonological alexia in which nonword reading is disrupted by a general phonological deficit that hurts nonwords more than words, phonological alexia would also arise if patients essentially could not read by the direct O→P network and were thus forced to rely on word meaning, as in deep dyslexia. In this case, however, there should be an accompanying deficit of word reading, and of a highly specific kind. In Friedman's view, (1) the word type least likely to allow reading via meaning is function words; and (2) one task indicative of a phonological deficit is nonword repetition. She therefore predicted that phonological alexic patients with a general phonological deficit should have an associated impairment in nonword repetition but no special problem with function words, whereas the other type should make errors on function words but manage adequate nonword repetition. LB (Derouesné & Beauvois, 1985), described earlier, was impaired at function-word reading but not nonword repetition. In her review of the cases in the literature with sufficient data to permit assignment to one of these two types, Friedman duly assigned LB to the semantic-route variant of phonological alexia.

Although two additional patients were given the same classification by Friedman (1995) on the basis of reasonably good nonword repetition (RG: Beauvois & Derouesné, 1979; AM: Patterson, 1982), this might be insufficient grounds to rule out a phonological deficit. A number of phonological alexic patients with adequate nonword repetition perform very poorly at the task of blending spoken segments into a fluent nonword pronunciation (Berndt et al., 1996; Patterson & Marcel, 1992); and the blending task may bear greater similarity than nonword repetition does to the phonological production stage of nonword reading. This might leave LB (Derouesné & Beauvois, 1985) as the only real candidate for the semantic variant of phonological alexia.

Phonological alexia has, of course, been of interest to reading researchers primarily for the insights it may provide into the processes of reading. Berndt et al. (1996) have argued that this disorder can inform theories of reading even if virtually all cases do have disrupted phonological processing in non-reading tasks. Why, then, has the introductory section of this chapter focused principally on the extent to which phonological alexia is explicable in terms of a more general language deficit? Even if the claim by Berndt et al. is accepted, one could still argue that a patient whose phonological alexia cannot be subsumed under a broader phonological deficit is more directly relevant to at least some debates about the structure of the reading system. After LB (Derouesné & Beauvois, 1985), the case to be presented here, CJ, may be the best example thus far of such a patient. He managed some (even if not a normal degree of) success on phonological processing in non-orthographic tasks, yet his nonword reading was very poor. Furthermore, an account of his pattern of word reading performance, even more than LB's, seems to require factors beyond a general phonological weakness.

The major issue that will be explored with reference to data from CJ is a debate about the nature of "word-specific" reading, using the following logic. Setting aside, for the moment, the procedure that computes a letter-string's pronunciation on the basis of some generalisable knowledge (in the Coltheart et al., 1993 model, this is a set of non-lexical grapheme–phoneme correspondence rules; in the contrasting view of Friedman, 1995 and Plaut et al., 1996, this is a network of knowledge that is sensitive to the frequency of sub- and whole-word spelling patterns as well as to spelling–sound consistency): What reading procedure(s) remain? According to Berndt et al. (1996), Besner and Smith (1992), Coltheart et al. (1993), Funnell (1983), and many other theorists, two pathways remain: a lexical, non-semantic route that links a familiar word's orthographic form directly to its phonological form, and a semantic reading route. In the contrasting position, the former "lexical" knowledge is embodied in the direct O→P pathway, and thus only a semantic route remains (O→S→P). If a phonological alexic patient's poor nonword reading cannot be adequately explained by a more general phonological deficit, and instead suggests that the "generalisable" procedure is largely unusable, then it seems that such a patient's reading performance might be informative about the debate over a lexical, non-semantic route.

CASE REPORT

CJ was given his nickname "the Singing Detective" because (1) he was, prior to his stroke, a policeman; (2) both before and after his stroke, he was a keen singer and member of a police choir; and (3) around the time of this study, BBC television was screening a popular serialised version of Dennis Potter's *The Singing Detective*. Born in 1931, CJ suffered a left middle-cerebral artery stroke in 1981; this apparently resulted in reasonably severe receptive and expressive aphasia, which had resolved to a considerable extent by the time that he was first tested by Funnell (in about 1985, published in Funnell, 1987); the data reported here were collected in 1990–91.[2] Funnell's initial study, devoted to issues about the impact of morphological word structure on reading, described CJ as right-handed, on the basis of his writing; but further interrogation revealed that he had—like many of his generation—been forced to write with his right hand at school. By preference, CJ would have written with his left hand, and continued to prefer his left hand for other tasks requiring fine motor control. His cerebral infarct (not thoroughly investigated neurologically) was on the left, and his initial aphasia certainly suggests left-hemisphere lateralisation of language function; but his left-handedness raises at least the possibility that his good language recovery was attributable to some degree of bilateral representation. It is also interesting to note that several other cases of phonological alexia have had an atypical pattern of laterality/side of lesion: both LB (Derouesné & Beauvois, 1985) and "Leonardo" (Job & Sartori, 1984) were right-handed with right-hemisphere lesions, whereas AM (Patterson, 1982) was left-handed with a right-hemisphere CVA. Whether these atypical cases amount to a higher than expected proportion, and what it would mean if they did, is unclear.

At the time of this investigation, CJ had good speech comprehension, at least in normal conversational situations; it was not formally retested following the earlier assessment that he had good comprehension "for all but the most complex syntactic constructions" (Funnell, 1987, p. 501). His speech was fluent in the sense of grammatically adequate (certainly no frank agrammatism) but rather slow in pace and somewhat hesitant, possibly due to occasional word-finding difficulty, though there was no striking anomia (confirmed later by his good success in object/picture naming). As is common with left perisylvian damage, one of CJ's most prominent and persistent post-insult deficits was in auditory-verbal short-term memory: his digit span was two items.

---

[2] Elaine Funnell kindly provided access to the patient, and the present study was in fact a collaborative venture between KP and EF. The chapter is not dual-authored because we did not entirely agree on the interpretation of the results obtained and, to avoid an untidy discussion section, we elected amicably to present KP's version.

EXPERIMENTAL INVESTIGATIONS

The focus of these investigations was the nature of CJ's *word* reading—the factors that modulated its success and the implication of the pattern of effects for theories of normal reading. Funnell's (1987) assessment of a substantial *nonword* reading impairment was confirmed with one nonword reading test, but this aspect of CJ's performance was not extensively investigated in this study. The results will be organised into four sections: (1) nonword reading; (2) phonological abilities; (3) accuracy and speed of word reading as a function of several variables; and (4) a comparison between word reading and object naming.

Nonword reading

CJ was asked to read a list of 48 monosyllabic, 4–5 letter, orthographically well-formed nonwords (from Patterson & Marcel, 1992), in which half of the items were "ordinary" nonwords and half were pseudohomophones— that is, the way in which the majority of readers would pronounce each pseudohomophonic nonword corresponds to the pronunciation of a real word.[3] The list was actually composed of 24 pairs, each consisting of one ordinary nonword and one pseudohomophone with the same orthographic "body", such as *teace/leace* and *broe/gloe*. The list of 48 items was randomised, except for ensuring that the two body-matched members of a pair were well separated. The items were presented to CJ, each nonword printed on a separate card, for untimed reading.

He read 10/48 (21%) of the nonwords correctly. Amongst his 10 correct responses, 4 were to ordinary nonwords and 6 to pseudohomophones, thus yielding no evidence of a significant advantage for nonwords with familiar pronunciations. Of his 38 incorrect responses, the majority, 23 responses, were productions of a single orthographically/phonologically similar real word, e.g. *werk*→"week", *roond*→"room", *wune*→"wine", *muve*→ "mauve". In many instances, CJ indicated that he knew that these word productions were wrong by saying, after his response, "but it's not" or "but it's wrong" or "that's all I can think of". The remaining incorrect trials consisted of nine failures to give any response at all; three

---

[3] Although the degree of orthographic resemblance of pseudohomophones to their base words has been shown to modulate the pseudohomophone advantage in nonword reading in some cases of phonological alexia (see Howard & Best, 1996, for example), this factor was not systematically manipulated here. Some of the pseudohomophones differed from their base words by a single letter in the same position (e.g. *werk* from *work*), whereas others were more orthographically discrepant (e.g. *toom* from *tomb*).

orthographically and phonologically similar nonword responses (e.g. *duve*→/dul/); and three responses based on a kind of orthographic and/or phonological segmentation (*teace*→"tea ... ace ... trace"; *soam*→"so ... am"; *smair*→"air ... but an S in front ... /sƏmeƏ/").

This clearly represents a significant degree of failure to read nonwords, though not to the extent reported for CJ previously (0/10) by Funnell (1987). Since the items tested were similar but not identical, (for example, Funnell's set of 10 included no pseudohomophones), one cannot conclude definitively that this difference reflects an improvement in CJ's nonword reading in the approximately 6 years between the two studies; but it might. Furthermore, with only two exceptions, every one of CJ's (non-omission) responses to the current nonword set contained the correct initial phoneme, even if it was not the same orthographic letter (e.g. *jerm*→"gem", *neen*→"knee"). The two exceptions to this generalisation were *wite*→"write", and one case where his response was very orthographically —but interestingly, perhaps not so phonologically—discrepant from the target, *hoaze*→"ozone is all I can think of". This is not compelling evidence of knowledge of the sounds of letters, but once again might suggest some slight recovery relative to Funnell's (1987) report that CJ failed utterly to sound individual letters (0/12). Unfortunately, his single-letter sounding was not reassessed in the later phase of testing.

This limited assessment of nonword reading suggests four conclusions: (1) CJ's skill at nonword reading was severely abnormal; (2) his performance was not facilitated by phonological familiarity of the response; (3) it is possible that his nonword reading had improved somewhat from the earlier total failure reported by Funnell (1987); and therefore (4) in drawing conclusions about the nature of CJ's *word* reading, one should not necessarily assume zero contribution from the procedures that normally accomplish *nonword* reading.

Phonological abilities

CJ's nonword repetition, at least for simple monosyllabic 3–4 phoneme nonwords, was good though not perfect: 24/30 (80%), with five of his six errors being lexicalisations (e.g. "pite"[/paɪt/]→"pipe", "dind" [/dɪnd] →"din").

In a very simple phonological task of judging the number of syllables in a spoken word, CJ performed well (28/30 correct) on a list where the words varied from one syllable (e.g. "vague") to four (e.g. "capillary"); his two mistakes were to identify "prize" as having two syllables and "comparison" as having three.

CJ also performed well when asked to judge whether a pair of monosyllabic spoken words rhymed: 56/60 (93%), with two misses ("no" to a rhyming pair) and two false positives ("yes" to a non-rhyme).[4] By contrast to his good *detection* of spoken rhymes, which at least indicates that he understood the concept, CJ was extremely poor at rhyme *production*. A test with 24 monosyllabic target words was aborted after eight trials, not because of his failure rate (1/8 correct) but because the task was so arduous for him. He was willing to keep trying on each target, repeating the stimulus word over and over, and sometimes producing a phrase (e.g. "pine"→"pine, pine, I keep thinking of pine-tree"). Despite numerous examples of acceptable responses from the experimenter, however, he could not succeed, and volunteered the intuition that this was because he could not get the sound of the stimulus word out of his head. On a further eight trials with only the rime (without its initial consonant) of a target word as spoken stimulus (e.g. "ain" from *rain*), he managed 3/8 correct responses (e.g. "air" [from *chair*] →"fair"). If normal rhyme production requires both phonological segmentation of the stimulus and phonological blending of the response, this might suggest that CJ was slightly helped if the task required only the blending operation; but 3/8 still represents a substantial impairment.

Table 3.1 details CJ's performance on the phonological manipulation tasks of segmentation and blending from Patterson and Marcel (1992). In the segmentation test, CJ was given a spoken monosyllabic word or nonword and asked to delete the initial sound and say what remained; in the blending test, the presentation consisted of a single spoken initial phoneme followed by a rime, and the task was to concatenate the two and say the resulting monosyllabic response. In both tasks, the major manipulation was the lexical status of the response: On half of both the 48 segmentation and 48 blending trials, the outcome was a real word and on half a nonword. All six of the phonological alexic patients tested by Patterson and Marcel were significantly impaired on one or both of these tests, and four of the six showed a significant advantage for word over nonword responses on the blending test.

CJ found these tasks difficult; in blending he often requested multiple presentations of the segments before attempting a response, and in segmentation, he also tended to repeat each stimulus aloud several times before responding; and in both tasks, he occasionally produced one or more erroneous responses before self-correcting. As revealed in Table 3.1, if one used

---

[4] This list (from Patterson, Vargha-Khadem, & Polkey, 1989), which was designed to be used also as a test of written-word rhyme detection, was composed of one-quarter each of the following four types: (1) orthographically similar rhymes (e.g. *pipe–ripe*), (2) orthographically dissimilar rhymes (*search–church*), (3) orthographically similar non-rhymes (e.g. *touch–couch*), (4) orthographically dissimilar non-rhymes (*wall–yell*). The fact that all of CJ's errors were to items where one would be misled by the orthography (i.e. pairs from conditions 2 and 3) might suggest some knowledge of/reference to orthographic information in this task (Seidenberg & Tanenhaus, 1979), but the number of errors is really too small to interpret.

TABLE 3.1
CJ's performance in phonological segmentation and blending
(tests from Patterson & Marcel, 1992)

	No. of Responses			
	Initially correct	*Subsequently correct*	*Never correct*	*Total*
Segmentation				
Word response	18	1	5	24
Nonword response	16	2	6	24
Blending				
Word response	14	6	4	24
Nonword response	10	10	4	24

The stimuli are designed such that a correct phonological operation (segmentation or blending) will result in a real word response on half of the trials and a nonword response on the other half.

a stringent scoring criterion of requiring the first response to be correct, then the judgement would have to be that CJ was poor at these phonological manipulations, especially blending. By the more lenient criterion of accepting as correct any trial where he eventually achieved the correct response, however, this does not represent a severe impairment, especially relative to some other reported phonological alexic patients (see for example Berndt et al., 1996 as well as Patterson & Marcel, 1992). Furthermore, CJ's success in both tasks was essentially as high for nonword as for word responses. One could certainly not conclude that CJ's phonological skills in non-reading tasks were normal; but given that he *failed* to produce a correct response to about 80% of simple nonwords in reading, his roughly 80% *correct* performance in both segmentation and blending even with nonword responses suggests that a general phonological weakness impeding the production of unfamiliar phonological forms may not provide an adequate explanation of his nonword reading deficit.

Word reading

Introduction and methods.   The structure of this assessment was determined by the assumption that major effects of three specific variables constitute "signatures" of different components of the reading process. The first variable of interest is a semantic manipulation: Imageable and/or concrete content words are generally thought to have an advantage over both abstract content words and function words in the richness and specificity of semantic representations, and therefore in the success and speed with which they can activate corresponding phonological representations for speech (Breedin, Saffran, & Coslett, 1994; Plaut & Shallice, 1993; Strain, Patterson, & Seidenberg, 1995). A demonstration that CJ's reading performance was modulated by this kind of semantic variable would indicate that activation of word meaning makes a major contribution to his reading. Funnell (1987), in her earlier investigation of CJ, reported that he was more successful in oral reading of high- than low-imageability words, but gave more theoretical prominence to the significant frequency effects in his reading performance (see later).

Second, an impact of spelling–sound regularity is standardly taken to reflect a major contribution of the procedure that computes phonology directly from orthography in a fashion that is sensitive to general character-istics of correspondences across the vocabulary. As noted in the Introduction, in the model of Coltheart et al. (1993), this is a non-lexical GPC procedure; in the contrasting view of Plaut et al. (1996), this is a network of knowledge that is sensitive to the frequency of whole-word spelling patterns as well as to spelling–sound consistency. Although the view adopted in this chapter is the latter, for this purpose it does not greatly matter which theoretical framework one prefers. If it can be shown that CJ's reading performance is largely insensitive to spelling–sound regularity, this would argue against a major contribution to his reading of the procedure that is sensitive to sub-word consistency or regularity.

The final variable included in these assessments, word frequency, may be less specifically diagnostic than the other two because (as argued persua-sively by Monsell, Doyle, & Haggard, 1989) frequency may well modulate the success or efficiency of multiple stages of word processing. A major impact of word frequency in reading certainly suggests the operation of some procedure that is more influenced by whole-word patterns than by the typicality or regularity of sub-word components, and has sometimes been associated more specifically with a visual word-form recognition system. On the assumption that a degree of damage to this system would impair recogni-tion of lower-frequency written words, a major accuracy advantage for high frequency words has been nominated as the signature of the (partially intact) lexical-nonsemantic procedure (Coltheart, 1985; Coltheart et al., 1993; Funnell, 1987). This was the interpretation of CJ provided by Funnell (1987). In that study, Funnell contrasted CJ with JG, a deep dyslexic patient with the defining "deep" symptom of single-word semantic errors in oral reading (e.g. *dream*→"fantasy"). Both patients were more successful on high- than low-imageability words, but only CJ showed a robust advantage for words of high frequency.

Speed as well as accuracy measures are presented for the majority of tests reported later; in these cases, the words were presented on the screen of a Macintosh Plus computer (in lower case, 24-point type), and CJ's response times were measured with a voice key and the PsychLab program (Gum & Bub, 1988). CJ's reading responses were slow, and the sort of presentation typically used in timed word-naming experiments with normal subjects would have risked losing a number of RT observations, because CJ's response to word N would sometimes overlap with presentation of word $N+1$. A rather leisurely pace of stimulus presentation was therefore employed. A typical trial consisted of the following sequence: a 1000msec fixation point, followed by a 500msec pause, and then an exposure of the target word which was terminated by the voice key if CJ responded within 5000msec but by disappearance of the word after this period if he did not. A further 500msec pause ensued before the fixation point for the next trial appeared.

Two factors complicate the interpretation of RT measures in a single-case study. First, RT differences shown by normal readers (in the difference, for example, between words with a typical/atypical spelling–sound correspondence) tend to be small and, although characteristic of group data, not necessarily true of every individual in the group (e.g. Bernstein & Carr, 1996; Strain et al., 1998). Unless one knows that a particular patient, premorbidly, had a robust effect,[5] the absence of a significant effect in a single case is therefore not very meaningful. Second, the speed of a patient's responses is often not only slower but substantially more variable than that of normal controls, with the result that mean differences may appear large but fail to reach conventional levels of significance. In general, therefore, the RT measures for CJ's reading will be presented here (1) as a general indication of his efficiency in word reading, and (2) as a rough guide to factors that may speed or slow his responses; but differences will not be tested for reliability and not given substantial weight. The standard way in which the RT data were handled was to remove all trials on which either (1) CJ's response was incorrect; (2) his latency to respond was greater than 2500msec (typically about 2–3 standard deviations beyond his mean, and substantially beyond the normal range); or (3) the voice key was triggered by something other than his intended response, e.g. if he started to say an incorrect word before self-correcting, or coughed or said "er ...". Means and standard deviations were then calculated for the remaining "good" trials.

Results.   Tables 3.2, 3.3, 3.4, and 3.5 present data on a variety of word lists, each designed to assess the impact of one, two, or all three of the variables outlined previously. The two tests in Table 3.2, each of which had just two conditions, demonstrate a sizeable advantage in the accuracy of CJ's reading for (1) highly imageable and concrete nouns relative to nouns low on both of these dimensions, and (2) content words relative to function words. There is also a suggestion that correct responses were slower to the

---

[5] In this regard, there is a real advantage to longitudinal studies of patients with neurodegenerative disease that can begin when the patient is at a mild stage of impairment (see for example Funnell, 1996; Strain et al., 1998; Tyler, Moss, Patterson, & Hodges, 1996).

TABLE 3.2
CJ's reading performance on two lists of words designed to assess effects of a semantic manipulation

	Accuracy	Mean RT (msec)	SD
Imageability/concreteness[a]			
High imageability/high concreteness	65/76 (0.86)	1097.9*	400.7
Low imageability/low concreteness	42/76 (0.55)	1320.4*	476.1
Content/function words[b]			
Content	57/60 (0.95)	—	—
Function	39/60 (0.65)	—	—

[a]One-syllable nouns matched for frequency, length, and initial phoneme (imageability/ concreteness ratings from the MRC DataBase, Coltheart, 1981).[b] One-syllable words matched for length; average word frequency was higher for function than content word set includes many of the commonest words in the language (e.g. *them, once, which*); but the content words were selected to be of the highest possible frequency (e.g. *year, high, place*) (from Patterson, 1979).
*Based on correct responses with an RT ≤ 2500msec.

abstract than the concrete nouns, though his RTs here as elsewhere were generally rather slow and variable. The first two lists in Table 3.3, both of which included a manipulation of imageability, also revealed a prominent decrease in CJ's word-reading success when the words were of low rather than high imageability.

The second variable in the first list of Table 3.3, regularity of spelling–sound correspondences, had essentially no impact on CJ's reading success: for high-imageability words, the proportions of correct responses to the two regularity conditions were identical, and for low-imageability items, the slight numerical advantage for regular words was not significant, χ^2 (1 df) = 0.59, P = 0.44. Latency measures also yielded no regularity effect: The mean difference at high imageability, though favouring regular words, was very small relative to the standard deviations; and the slightly larger, though still smallish, mean RT difference at low imageability went in the wrong direction: regular words slower, not faster, than irregular words.

The second variable in Table 3.3, word frequency, yielded both a large main effect and an interaction with imageability: CJ's performance was dramatically poor for words low on both dimensions (the number of correct responses in this condition was sufficiently small that the RT measure, based on so few observations, should not be given any weight). Interestingly, CJ was tested (for accuracy, though not latency) on this same list of words about 6 years before the current assessment, with the results published in Funnell (1987). On the earlier occasion, and given here in the same order as the conditions in list two of Table 3.3, CJ correctly named 1.00, 0.87, 0.74, and 0.26 of the word sets: an extraordinary degree of reproduceability over a 6-year gap.

TABLE 3.3

CJ's reading performance (accuracy and speed) on three lists of words each designed to assess the impact of two variables

	Accuracy	Mean RT* (msec)	(SD)
Imageability × regularity[a]			
High imageability, regular	62/65 (0.95)	1176.7	459.7
High imageability, irregular	62/65 (0.95)	1213.7	462.8
Low imageability, regular	33/55 (0.60)	1385.9	523.4
Low imageability, irregular	29/55 (0.53)	1279.0	386.4
Imageability × frequency[b]			
High imageability, high frequency	37/38 (0.97)	998.1	153.2
High imageability, low frequency	34/38 (0.89)	1244.4	263.8
Low imageability, high frequency	27/38 (0.71)	1299.3	291.6
Low imageability, low frequency	8/38 (0.21)	1524.0	211.9
Regularity × frequency[c]			
Regular, high frequency	37/42 (0.88)	1117.6	274.3
Irregular, high frequency	30/41 (0.73)	1146.3	228.7
Regular, medium frequency	33/42 (0.79)	1286.0	498.9
Irregular, medium frequency	33/42 (0.79)	1161.1	310.7
Regular, low frequency	22/42 (0.52)	1412.9	477.4
Irregular, low frequency	27/42 (0.64)	1267.8	417.9

[a] One–two syllable words: all four conditions matched for frequency and length; regular/irregular sets matched for imageability (from Howard & Franklin, 1988). [b] One–three syllable nouns; two imageability sets matched for frequency and vice versa (from Funnell, 1987). [c] One-syllable words matched for length and initial phoneme; regular/irregular sets matched for frequency (from Patterson & Hodges, 1992).
*Based on correct responses with an RT ≤ 2500msec.

The final list in Table 3.3 assessed the joint impact of regularity and frequency, and produced a rather less neat result than the tests just described. CJ's accuracy declined with decreasing word frequency, though with a larger effect of frequency on regular than exception words: Normal readers produce the opposite pattern. There was a numerical (but not significant) advantage for regular words at high frequency and one for exception words at low frequency: again, highly atypical of normal readers. Averaged over the three frequency bands, CJ correctly named 0.73 of the regular and 0.72 of the irregular words, confirming the result from the first list that there was no main effect of regularity on accuracy. The RT results more or less mirror the accuracy data: a small, non-significant advantage for regular words at high frequency, and mean differences favouring the exception words (again not substantial relative to the standard deviations) in the lower frequency bands. CJ's generally rather poor accuracy on this list probably reflects the fact that the list contains a low proportion of concrete nouns, the type of word that he was most likely to read correctly.

The third list in Table 3.3 offers the opportunity to assess the degree of CJ's slowness in word-naming response times. A group of normal control subjects (age-matched to a group of patients with early Alzheimer's disease, and thus a reasonable age match for CJ) produced mean RTs for the various conditions of this identical list between 650msec (for high-frequency regular words) and 680msec (low-frequency irregular words) (Strain et al., 1998). CJ's responses were on average nearly twice as long.

Tables 3.4 and 3.5 provide the final assessment in this section, a list of words manipulating all three variables of imageability, frequency, and regularity of spelling–sound correspondences (described in Funnell, 1996). Given the difficulties of creating such a list in which the contrasting words on each dimension are matched on the other two, the list contains only 11 words/condition. CJ was therefore asked to read this list of words twice (on two occasions, separated by about a month) in order to increase the number of observations per cell for the accuracy measure; RTs were collected on only one of these two occasions. Table 3.4 shows his proportion of correct responses for each of the eight conditions separately (out of a total of $N = 22$, i.e. 2 occasions × 11 words). For a clearer indication of the effect of each of the three variables on both accuracy and speed, the data are then presented in Table 3.5 for the "high" and "low" sub-sets of each dimension, collapsed across the other two. A log-linear analysis of CJ's accuracy across the different conditions yielded a highly reliable advantage for high > low imageability, χ^2 (1 df) $= 26.79$, $P < .001$, and a marginal advantage for high > low frequency, χ^2 (1 df) $= 3.67$, $P = .056$. There was no effect of regularity, and no significant interaction between any of the variables; imageability × frequency produced χ^2 (1 df) $= 2.31$, $P = .13$, and the remaining χ^2 values were all   1.0.

TABLE 3.4
CJ's accuracy (proportion corre) in each of the eight separate conditions of a set of 1–2 syllable words varying orthogonally in imageability, frequency and regularity (stimulus list from Funnell, 1996).

High Imageability				Low Imageability			
High Frequency		Low Frequency		High Frequency		Low Frequency	
Regular	Irregular	Regular	Irregular	Regular	Irregular	Regular	Irregular
.87	.96	.96	.91	.73	.73	.50	.45

TABLE 3.5

CJ's accuracy (number and proportion correct) and speed (mean RT in msec) for the list of items from Table 3.4, as a function of each of the three manipulated variables

	High			Low		
	Accuracy	*RT*	*N*	*Accuracy*	*RT*	*N*
Imageability	81/88 (0.92)	972.5	36	54/88 (0.61)	1185.4	22
Frequency	72/88 (0.82)	1045.2	33	62/88 (0.71)	1063.9	25
Regularity	67/88 (0.76)	982.0	29	67/88 (0.76)	1124.6	29

For ease of presentation in these summaries, regular and irregular words are labelled "high" and "low" Regularity. RTs were measured only on one occasion; *N* for RT is the number of responses on which each mean RT is based, excluding errors and responses > 2500ms.

The nature of CJ's reading errors.   The data in Tables 3.2, 3.3, 3.4, and 3.5 represent over 1000 individual word-reading responses by CJ. Of his incorrect responses, not a single one could be construed as an unequivocal semantic error of the kind made by deep dyslexic patients (Coltheart et al., 1980), such as *sick*→"ill", *nephew*→"cousin" or *hermit*→"recluse". CJ failed to make any response at all on some small proportion of trials, more notably with low-imageability words like *cause* and *cite*, and more often in the somewhat time-pressured context of RT measurements than he would do in unpaced, over-the-desk reading. He also made some responses that could be described as morphological errors, such as *goes*→"going", *kept*→"keep" and *called*→"calling" (though see Funnell's 1987 judgement that such errors can be adequately explained without any assumptions about separate representation of root and bound morphemes). The vast majority of his errors—perhaps the only really significant category in terms of numbers of exemplars—were produc-tions of another real word bearing some substantial orthographic and in some cases also phonological resemblance to the target word (e.g. *doubt*→ "double", *debut*→"debt", *grown*→"gown", *wicker*→"wicket", *candid*→ "candy"). These seem explicable on the twin assumptions (1) that the process by which orthographic representations activate word meaning is a somewhat approxi-mate one, such that the letter string *candid* partially activates the semantic representation for *candy* as well as *candid*, and (2) that a more common and more concrete meaning like *candy* might well be more successful than the actual stimulus word, *candid*, at completing the process of phonological acti-vation for speech production. As with CJ's errors of commission to nonwords, his error responses to words—virtually without exception—preserved the first phoneme of the target word.

Word reading vs object naming

If one assumed that O→S→P activation formed a major component of the process by which CJ read words aloud, then a simplistic prediction might be the following: For words representing the names of objects, his reading performance should largely resemble his object naming performance. This is, of course, an over-simplification in more ways than one (see Howard, 1985 for discussion). For example, (1) any cognitive theory must acknowledge that the processes of stimulus analysis for written words and line drawings are different. (2) Semantic representations, even more than other kinds of representations (e.g. orthographic or phonological), must be flexibly computed rather than addressed in fixed form, and as such will tend to differ as a function of many variables, including the nature of the input. Even on the assumption that objects and words largely share representations at a semantic level (Caramazza, Hillis, Rapp, & Romani, 1990) rather than requiring separate semantic systems (McCarthy & Warrington, 1988), one might therefore expect a picture of a giraffe and the word *giraffe* to activate overlapping, but not identical, sets of semantic features (Lambon Ralph, Patterson, & Hodges, 1997). (3) Different conglomerates of semantic features may be differentially successful or efficient in activating the phonological representation of the name of the object/word.

Despite these three differences in the detailed nature of word and picture processing, it nonetheless seems that, if semantic activation plays a greater-than-normal role in a patient's reading, and furthermore if that patient has no deficit affecting either the orthographic processing of written words or the visuo-spatial processing of line drawings, then one might expect some similarities in his word reading and picture naming. Here, this prediction was addressed by an experiment on semantic priming of reading and naming. Groups of normal subjects show significant semantic priming effects in both tasks but typically of very different magnitudes, with significantly greater priming for picture naming than for word reading (see for example Bajo, 1988); this is presumably because reading aloud, even if facilitated by semantic processing, can rely to a large extent on direct O→P translation. If CJ's capacity for this kind of direct translation was largely inoperative, or at least very slow/inefficient/noisy, then he might be expected to show roughly equivalent priming effects in the two tasks.

Pre-test of object naming.   For the priming experiment itself, identical items were used in the reading and naming tasks; but as an initial evaluation of CJ's picture naming abilities, and also as a basis on which to select the stimuli for the priming experiment, he was asked to name the 260 line drawings of common objects from Snodgrass and Vanderwart (1980; hereinafter S&V). Furthermore, not because there was any intrinsic interest in his speeded picture naming, but because the priming experiment would require limited stimulus exposure for RT measurements on pictures as well as words, he was asked to name the 260 line drawings under essentially identical conditions to those described earlier for timed word reading. That is, the line drawings were presented on the screen of a Macintosh computer for a maximum of 5000msec (plus additional shorter durations for pre-stimulus fixation, inter-trial interval, etc., as detailed earlier). The 260 pictures were randomised and then divided into six blocks of either 44 or 43 items each; CJ was given a rest break of a minute or two between blocks.

Under these conditions, CJ's first response was a correct name for the picture on 195/260, or 0.75, of the S&V line drawings. Since there are no data for his reading of the names of the full S&V set, one cannot assert that he named the pictures as successfully as he would have read the words. Indeed, his word-reading performance on concrete nouns (Tables 3.2–3.5) does suggest better reading than naming, even allowing for the fact that the names of some of the S&V pictures are both longer and lower in frequency than many of the words employed in the reading tests. His 75% correct naming score does, however, represent good success: many aphasic patients perform less well even without time pressure. The majority of his errors (N = 44 or 17% of total responses) were failures to produce any naming response (undoubtedly made more prevalent by the speeded conditions); the remaining 21 (8% of total responses) were semantically related responses (e.g. fly→"wasp", strawberry→"apple", mitten→"glove", toe→"thumb", blouse→"coat", etc.), including a couple of superordinate terms (eagle→ "bird", flower→"plant"). He sometimes made it clear that he knew that his semantic errors were wrong, and occasionally even managed to self-correct within the trial interval, though again the timing constraints undoubtedly worked against him in this regard. Normal subjects make some semantic errors in speeded naming of line drawings, too (see Vitkovitch & Humphreys, 1991, for example). A group of elderly normal subjects tested in Cambridge, UK (as controls for a study of patients with Alzheimer's disease: see Hodges & Patterson, 1995; Strain et al., 1998) were asked to name 48 line drawings from the S&V set under time pressure to enable RT measurements; their rate of semantic errors was in fact higher than CJ's 8%, athough they had fewer omissions.

Priming experiment. Twenty-four target items were selected from the S&V set that (1) CJ had named correctly and promptly from the line drawing, (2) had a monomorphemic name (i.e. ruling out double-barrelled names like *rolling pin* or *doorknob*), and (3) had a strongly associated, monomorphemic word from the same semantic category, to be used as a prime picture or word. This procedure yielded pairs (given in the order prime–target) such as *horse–cow*; *tie–shirt*; *swan–duck*; *cigar–pipe*;

sheep–goat). Over a period of a month, CJ was given four experimental sessions; in two of these he named a given target item to its picture and in the other two in response to the written word; within each modality, on one occasion the target was preceded by its own associate (e.g. *swan–duck*) and on the other by the associate of a different, unrelated, target item (e.g. *cigar–duck*). Each experimental session was entirely within modality, both across targets and between primes and targets: that is, on a given session, CJ either named a set of target pictures, each preceded by a related or unrelated picture prime, or else read a set of words, each preceded by a related or unrelated word prime.

CJ was instructed that he would see a sequence of pairs of items (either words or pictures); the first item in each pair would appear rather briefly, and he was asked only to look at this, not to respond to it in any way; the second item of the pair would appear and stay on the screen longer, and he was to read the word (or say the name of the picture). He was given plenty of practice with this procedure at the start of each session (using associated and unassociated pairs that were not part of the real prime–target set), and he had no difficulty understanding and following these instructions.

Each trial consisted of the following sequence of events (with their exposure durations in brackets): fixation point (1000msec), ISI-1 (500msec), prime (related or unrelated word or picture) (1000msec), ISI-2 (500msec), target (maximum of 5000msec, but erased by response if earlier than 5000msec); ITI (500 msec).

Although the obvious intention was to have four valid responses to each target (i.e. correct reading/naming with related/unrelated prime, RT $\leq$ 2500msec in all cases), this goal was overly optimistic; of the 24 quartets of observations, 8/24 contained one case that failed to satisfy these criteria. Since the properly balanced design requires all four conditions, only the 16 target items with "good" observations for all four conditions were included in the analysis. The results for this set (mean RTs for unrelated, related, and the difference between them, unrelated–related) are displayed in the top half of Table 3.6, and reveal substantial priming effects for both modalities. Although it might look as if the priming was slightly greater for pictures than words, this is almost certainly related to the fact that—over the whole set of 16 items—the mean RT for picture naming in the unrelated condition was slower (by 237msec) than the mean RT for word naming in the unrelated condition; slower responses give more "room" for facilitation. Indeed, if one removes the 6/16 stimuli where CJ's responses in the two unrelated conditions were more than 150msec longer to the picture than to the corresponding word, leaving ten items with reasonably comparable RTs to words and pictures in the unrelated conditions (the second set of data in Table 3.6), then in fact the priming effect was numerically *larger* for reading than naming.

TABLE 3.6
CJ's mean RTs in the various conditions of the priming experiment

	Prime		
	Unrelated	*Related*	*U–R*
Word (*n* = 16)			
Mean RT (msec)	1041.8	909.0	131.9
SD	201.7	124.8	
Picture (*n* = 16)			
Mean RT (msec)	1278.9	1104.1	174.8
SD	292.1	252.4	
Word (*n* = 10)			
Mean RT (msec)	1056.0	905.1	150.9
SD	179.6	103.1	
Picture (*n* = 10)			
Mean RT (msec)	1136.0	1011.4	124.6
SD	173.9	148.0	

A detailed discussion of semantic priming effects (how they arise, at what level(s) they occur, whether different kinds of semantic relationships demand different accounts, etc) is beyond the scope of this chapter. Suffice it to say that, since CJ showed as much semantic priming in reading a word as in naming a picture, it seems very likely that activation of semantic representations played a major role in his word reading.

CONCLUSIONS

Like most individual studies, the results from this one suggest, rather than unequivocally establishing, some interpretations and theoretical implications. There are at least two reasons for such caution in drawing conclusions. The first is a data limitation: This study provided a considerable quantity of data on CJ's reading, picture naming, phonological processing, etc.; nonetheless, many relevant issues would only be addressable with still further observations. The second is a limitation in theory: the models with which we work are often under-specified in ways that make it difficult to interpret results precisely, or indeed even to know whether apparently different theoretical positions actually make critically different predictions. Despite these caveats, the conclusions listed here will be stated in reasonably strong terms, partly because they are more falsifiable in such terms, and partly because strong positions are more thought-provoking than statements hedged about with qualifications.

To begin with the issue that dominated much of the introduction to this chapter: Although CJ's pattern of word and nonword reading does not seem interpretable solely in terms of a general phonological weakness, he almost certainly had a phonological deficit that transcends the reading process. He was slow, and made errors, on the separate tasks of phonological segmentation and blending; and he was virtually unable to do rhyme production, a task that might be viewed as requiring both segmentation and blending. The precise nature of this deficit, and how, for example, it relates to the impaired phonological short-term memory of all reported cases of phonological alexia (see Bisiacchi et al., 1989 and Friedman, 1996 for discussion of this issue) is not completely clear. What does seem clear is that, although this kind of general phonological deficit was a less prominent feature for CJ (as well as LB: Derouesné & Beauvois, 1985, and RR: Bisiacchi et al., 1989) than for the majority of cases in the literature, no case has yet been reported with a strong word/nonword dissociation in reading but normal abilities in the domain of phonological tasks without any orthographic component. There has, as yet, been no convincing challenge to the suggestion by Farah et al. (1996) and Patterson and Marcel (1992), that the emphasis in the label "phonological alexia" should be on the first rather than the second component of this label.

As a corollary of this first conclusion, it seems that Friedman's (1995) differentiation between two types of phonological alexia might warrant a little modification. Recall that Friedman distinguished between the following two patterns: (1) patients who are still able to translate O→P but, because of a weak phonological system that exacerbates the normal advantage for familiar phonological representations, show a marked lexicality effect in reading and other phonologically demanding tasks; (2) patients whose direct O→P procedure is so disrupted (or at least so slow and inefficient) that they are forced to rely on reading by O→S→P. This distinction, which represented an important advance in the understanding of phonological alexia, still seems largely apt. First of all, however, impaired nonword repetition (as a hallmark of the first type) and impaired function word reading (as a distinctive symptom of the second) might not be the best or only defining symptoms. Second, and more importantly, the two deficits are not mutually exclusive. CJ was impaired at function-word reading, and on this as well as other bases, he is described here as an example (indeed, perhaps the best example thus far in the literature) of Friedman's second pattern of phonological alexia. Nevertheless, he probably also had some degree of phonological weakness.

The conclusion that the O→S→P procedure played a prominent role in CJ's word reading is based on three findings: (1) the large and consistent impact of a semantic variable, word imageability, on his success in word naming; (2) the fact that his speed of word naming was substantially facilitated by semantic priming, indeed with roughly equivalent priming effects for word reading and picture naming; and (3) the fact that his word naming RTs were slow. The third of these observations is much less direct evidence than the first two: slowness could arise for a variety of reasons, whereas the impact of both imageability and priming seem specifically diagnostic of semantic involvement. Slow word naming is, however, at least consistent with this interpretation.

Despite the conclusion that CJ's reading relied to a large extent on his comprehension of the words to be read aloud, it is entirely plausible that he had some minimal information available from the direct O→P procedure. This claim, based on his poor but non-zero nonword reading and the fact that his errors of commission in both word and nonword reading virtually always preserved the initial phoneme of the target string, is important for two reasons. The first is that, if even a small amount of activation from O→P can summate with that from O→S→P, this might help to explain CJ's general levels of success in word reading. That is, the semantic "route"—which at its best is probably inadequate to achieve full word reading skill (Frost, 1996, Van Orden, Pennington, & Stone, 1990)—need not have been doing all the work. Second, there is still no complete consensus in the literature on deep dyslexia as to whether semantic errors in single-word reading reflect a semantic deficit or a natural imprecision in an O→S→P procedure forced to operate in isolation. It is, however, notable that CJ made no semantic errors in reading; and as suggested long ago by Newcombe and Marshall (1980), the most minimal O→P information, even about the sound of the first letter, could successfully prevent semantic errors such as *hermit*→"recluse".

The claim, then, is that CJ's pattern of reading performance is consistent with a "triangle" model of single-word processing (Plaut et al., 1996) and does not demand the hypothesis of a separate whole-word, lexical non-semantic reading procedure. In CJ's case the O→P procedure, which normally does most of the work in reading aloud both words and nonwords, was severely (though probably not totally) disrupted. As a result, CJ relied to a much greater extent on a largely intact, but by its nature inadequate, procedure of reading via meaning.

REFERENCES

Bajo, M.-T. (1988). Semantic facilitation with pictures and words. *Journal of Experimental Psychology: Learning, Memory, and Cognition*, *14*, 579–589.

Beauvois, M.-F., & Derouesné, J. (1979). Phonological alexia: Three dissociations. *Journal of Neurology, Neurosurgery and Psychiatry*, *42*, 1115–1124.

Behrmann, M., Plaut, D.C., & Nelson, J. (1998). A literature review and new data supporting an interactive account of letter-by-letter reading. *Cognitive Neuropsychology*, *15*, 7–51.

Berndt, R.S., Haendiges, A.N., Mitchum, C.C., & Wayland, S.C. (1996). An investigation of nonlexical reading impairments. *Cognitive Neuropsychology*, *13*, 763–801.

Bernstein, S.E., & Carr, T.H. (1996). Dual-route theories of pronouncing printed words: What can be learned from concurrent task performance? *Journal of Experimental Psychology: Learning, Memory, and Cognition*, *22*, 86–116.

Besner, D., & Smith, M. (1992). Basic processes in reading: Is the orthographic depth hypothesis sinking? In R. Frost & L. Katz (Eds), *Advances in psychology: Orthography, phonology, morphology, and meaning* (pp. 45–66). New York: North Holland.

Bisiacchi, P.S., Cipolotti, L., & Denes, G. (1989). Impairment in processing meaningless verbal material in several modalities: The relationship between short-term memory and phonological skills. *Quarterly Journal of Experimental Psychology, 41A*, 293–319.

Breedin, S.D., Saffran, E.M., & Coslett, H.B. (1994). Reversal of the concreteness effect in a patient with semantic dementia. *Cognitive Neuropsychology, 11*, 617–660.

Caramazza, A., Hillis, A.E., Rapp, B.C., & Romani. C. (1990). The multiple semantics hypothesis: Multiple confusions. *Cognitive Neuropsychology, 7*, 161–189.

Coltheart, M. (1981). The MRC psycholinguistic database. *Quarterly Journal of Experimental Psychology, 33A*, 497–505.

Coltheart, M. (1985). Cognitive neuropsychology and the study of reading. In M.I. Posner & O.S.M. Marin (Eds), *Attention and performance XI* (pp. 3–37). Hillsdale, NJ: Lawrence Erlbaum Associates Inc.

Coltheart, M. (1996) (Ed.) Phonological dyslexia [special issue]. *Cognitive Neuropsychology, 13*, 749–940.

Coltheart, M., Curtis, B., Atkins, P., & Haller, M. (1993). Models of reading aloud: Dual-route and parallel-distributed-processing approaches. *Psychological Review, 100*, 589–608.

Coltheart, M., Patterson, K., & Marshall, J.C. (Eds) (1980). *Deep dyslexia.* London: Routledge & Kegan Paul.

Derouesné, J., & Beauvois, M.-F. (1985). The "phonemic" stage in the nonlexical reading process: Evidence from a case of phonological alexia. In K. Patterson, J.C. Marshall, & M. Coltheart (Eds), *Surface dyslexia* (pp. 399–457). Hove, UK: Lawrence Erlbaum Associates Ltd.

Farah, M.J., Stowe, R.M., & Levinson, K.L. (1996). Phonological dyslexia: Loss of a reading-specific component of the cognitive architecture? *Cognitive Neuropsychology, 13*, 849–868.

Farah, M.J., & Wallace, M. (1991). Pure alexia as a visual impairment: A reconsideration. *Cognitive Neuropsychology, 8*, 313–334.

Friedman, R.B. (1995). Two types of phonological alexia. *Cortex, 31*, 397–403.

Friedman, R.B. (1996). Phonological text alexia: Poor pseudoword reading plus difficulty in reading functors and affixes in text. *Cognitive Neuropsychology, 13*, 869–885.

Friedman, R.B., & Alexander, M.P. (1984). Pictures, images, and pure alexia: A case study. *Cognitive Neuropsychology, 1*, 9–23.

Frost, R. (1996). Towards a strong phonological theory of reading: True issues and false trails. *Psychological Bulletin, 123*, 71–99.

Funnell, E. (1983). Phonological processes in reading: New evidence from acquired dyslexia. *British Journal of Psychology, 74*, 159–180.

Funnell, E. (1987). Morphological errors in acquired dyslexia: A case of mistaken identity. *Quarterly Journal of Experimental Psychology, 39A*, 497–539.

Funnell, E. (1996). Response biases in oral reading: An account of the co-occurrence of surface dyslexia and semantic dementia. *Quarterly Journal of Experimental Psychology, 49A*, 417–446.

Goldberg, E. (1995). Rise and fall of modular orthodoxy. *Journal of Clinical and Experimental Neuropsychology, 17*, 193–208.

Gum, T., & Bub, D. (1988). *Psychlab* [Computer program]. Montreal, Canada.

Hillis, A.E., & Caramazza, A. (1991). Mechanisms for accessing lexical representations for output: Evidence from a category specific semantic deficit. *Brain and Language, 40*, 106–144.

Hodges, J.R., & Patterson, K. (1995). Is semantic memory consistently impaired early in the course of Alzheimer's disease? Neuroanatomical and diagnostic implications. *Neuropsychologia, 33*, 441–459.

Howard, D. (1985). *The semantic organisation of the lexicon: Evidence from aphasia.* Unpublished PhD thesis, University of London, UK.

Howard, D., & Best, W. (1996). Developmental phonological dyslexia: Real word reading can be completely normal. *Cognitive Neuropsychology, 13,* 887–934.

Howard, D., & Franklin, S. (1988). *Missing the meaning? A cognitive neuropsychological study of processing of words by an aphasic patient.* Cambridge, MA: MIT Press.

Job, R., & Sartori, G. (1984). Morphological decomposition: Evidence from crossed phonological dyslexia. *Quarterly Journal of Experimental Psychology, 36A,* 435–458.

Lambon Ralph, M.A., Patterson, K., & Hodges, J.R. (1997). The relationship between naming and semantic knowledge for different categories in dementia of Alzheimer's type. *Neuropsychologia, 35,* 1251–1260.

Marshall, J.C., & Newcombe, F. (1973). Patterns of paralexia: A psycholinguistic approach. *Journal of Psycholinguistic Research, 2,* 175–199.

Masterson, J. (1985). On how we read nonwords: Data from different populations. In K. Patterson, J.C. Marshall, & M. Coltheart (Eds), *Surface dyslexia* (pp. 289–299). Hove, UK: Lawrence Erlbaum Associates Ltd.

McCarthy, R.A., & Warrington, E.K. (1988). Evidence for modality-specific meaning systems in the brain. *Nature, 334,* 428–430.

Monsell, S., Doyle, M.C., & Haggard, P.N. (1989). Effects of frequency on visual word recognition tasks: Where are they? *Journal of Experimental Psychology: General, 118,* 43–71.

Newcombe, F., & Marshall, J.C. (1980). Transcoding and lexical stabilization in deep dyslexia. In M. Coltheart, K. Patterson, & J.C. Marshall (Eds), *Deep dyslexia* (pp. 176–188). London: Routledge & Kegan Paul.

Patterson, K. (1979). What is right with deep dyslexic patients? *Brain and Language, 8,* 111–129.

Patterson, K. (1982). The relation between reading and phonological coding: Further neuropsychological observations. In A.W. Ellis (Ed.), *Normality and pathology in cognitive functions* (pp. 77–111). London: Academic Press.

Patterson, K., & Hodges, J.R. (1992). Deterioration of word meaning: Implications for reading. *Neuropsychologia, 30,* 1025–1040.

Patterson, K., & Marcel, A. (1992). Phonological ALEXIA or PHONOLOGICAL alexia? In J. Alegria, D. Holender, J. Junca de Morais, & M. Moreau (Eds), *Analytic approaches to human cognition* (pp. 259–274). Amsterdam: North Holland.

Patterson, K., Vargha-Khadem, F., & Polkey, C.E. (1989). Reading with one hemisphere. *Brain, 112,* 39–63.

Plaut, D.C., McClelland, J.L., Seidenberg, M.S., & Patterson, K. (1996). Understanding normal and impaired word reading: Computational principles in quasi-regular domains. *Psychological Review, 103,* 56–115.

Plaut, D.C., & Shallice, T. (1993). Deep dyslexia: A case study of connectionist neuropsychology. *Cognitive Neuropsychology, 10,* 377–500.

Seidenberg, M.S., & McClelland, J.L. (1989). A distributed, developmental model of word recognition and naming. *Psychological Review, 96,* 523–568.

Seidenberg, M.S., & Tanenhaus, M.K. (1979). Orthographic effects on rhyme monitoring. *Journal of Experimental Psychology: Human Learning and Memory, 5,* 546–554.

Sekuler, E.B., & Behrmann, M. (1996). Perceptual cues in pure alexia. *Cognitive Neuropsychology, 13,* 941–974.

Shallice, T. (1988). *From neuropsychology to mental structure.* Cambridge, UK: Cambridge University Press.

Shallice, T., & Warrington, E.K. (1980). Single and multiple component central dyslexic syndromes. In M. Coltheart, K. Patterson, & J.C. Marshall (Eds), *Deep dyslexia* (pp.

119–145). London: Routledge & Kegan Paul.

Snodgrass, J.G., & Vanderwart, M. (1980). A standardized set of 260 pictures: Norms for name agreement, image agreement, familiarity, and visual complexity. *Journal of Experimental Psychology: Human Learning and Memory*, *6*, 174–215.

Strain, E., Patterson, K., Graham, N., & Hodges, J.R. (1998). Word reading in Alzheimer's disease: Cross-sectional and longitudinal analyses of response time and accuracy data. *Neuropsychologia*, *36*, 155–171.

Strain, E., Patterson, K., & Seidenberg, M.S. (1995). Semantic effects in single-word naming. *Journal of Experimental Psychology: Learning, Memory and Cognition*, *21*, 1140–1154.

Tyler, L.K., Moss, H.E., Patterson, K., & Hodges, J.R. (1996). The gradual deterioration of syntax and semantics in a patient with progressive aphasia. *Brain and Language*, *56*, 426–476.

Van Orden, G.C., Pennington, B.F., & Stone, G.O. (1990). Word identification in reading and the promise of subsymbolic psycholinguistics. *Psychological Review*, *97*, 488–522.

Vitkovitch, M., & Humphreys, G.W. (1991). Perseverant responding in speeded naming of pictures: It's in the links. *Journal of Experimental Psychology: Learning, Memory, and Cognition*, *17*, 664–680.

CHAPTER FOUR

Surface dyslexia: Description, treatment, and interpretation

Andrew W. Ellis
Department of Psychology, University of York, UK

Matthew A. Lambon Ralph
Department of Psychology, University of York, UK; and MRC Cognition and Brain Sciences Unit, Cambridge, UK

Julie Morris
Department of Psychology, University of York, UK; and Department of Speech, University of Newcastle, UK

Alison Hunter
Speech and Language Therapy Department, Monkgate Health Centre, York, UK

INTRODUCTION

If the modern-day study of acquired dyslexia can be traced back to a single publication, it is to the journal article "Pattern of paralexia: A psycholinguistic approach" written by John Marshall and Freda Newcombe and published in 1973. A "paralexia" is simply a reading error, and Marshall and Newcombe used the errors made by patients with reading problems following brain injury to define and begin to explain three different forms of acquired dyslexia—*visual dyslexia* in which patients made purely "visual" errors such as reading DUG as "bug" and WAS as "saw", *deep dyslexia* in which patients made a variety of errors, most striking among which were "semantic" errors such as reading LITTLE as "small", DAUGHTER as "sister", and DIAMOND as "necklace", and *surface dyslexia*, which is the subject of this chapter.

Surface dyslexia was represented in the "Patterns of paralexia" article by two patients, JC and ST. The reading of both patients was characterised by laborious attempts to "sound out" words they would have been able to read with ease before their brain injuries. Often they misread words: examples of unsuccessful attempts to sound out once-familiar words are JC looking at ISLAND and saying "izland", and ST looking at PIGSTY and saying "pigisti". In both of these cases the patients were baffled as to what the word might mean.

Sometimes JC's and ST's attempts to read words happened to result in spoken responses that were not the target word but sounded like other real words. This invariably led to an incorrect guess as to the meaning of the word. For example, JC was tested at around the time that Cassius Clay (later Muhammad Ali) fought Sonny Liston for the World Heavyweight Boxing Championship. When he was shown the word LISTEN, JC read it as "liston" and added, "that's the boxer". On another occasion he misread BEGIN as "beggin", with the emphasis on the first syllable, and added, "collecting money" (see Newcombe & Marshall, 1981, for further instructive examples).

Marshall and Newcombe (1973) described their patients' error patterns and then sought to interpret their reading difficulties using a model of the normal reading process that leant heavily on the influential "logogen model" developed by John Morton (1969; 1970). They attempted to explain visual, surface, and deep dyslexia in terms of damage to processes which are required for normal, efficient word recognition. This is quintessentially the cognitive neuropsychological approach. Marshall and Newcombe also noted the similarities between the errors made frequently by their acquired dyslexics and the occasional errors of skilled readers, and the similarities between the errors of their acquired dyslexics and those of children with developmental dyslexia. In addition, they considered what form their three reading disorders might take in languages such as Japanese or Hebrew, which employ very different writing systems. These are all themes that have been extensively explored since, but as Marshall and Newcombe were at pains to point out, all had been the subject of discussion for the best part of a hundred years. Psychologists are bad at knowing about research done more than 5 years ago, but Marshall and Newcombe were fully aware that acquired dyslexia had been studied in considerable detail in the late 19th and early 20th centuries, and sporadically since. They knew that patients matching their categories of "visual", "surface" and "deep" dyslexia had been described and analysed by earlier investigators, and they directed the reader to the appropriate sources, whether in English, French, or German. "Patterns of paralexia" is a truly classic paper that anticipated many of the questions that have occupied cognitive neuropsychologists since. It should be on anyone's list of Desert Island Reprints.

THE CLASSIC SYMPTOMS OF SURFACE DYSLEXIA

The years following the publication of "Patterns of paralexia" witnessed a steady stream of publications on surface dyslexia, including a book, *Surface dyslexia: Neuropsychological and cognitive studies of phonological reading* edited by Patterson, Marshall, and Coltheart (1985). By the mid-1980s some degree of agreement had been reached as to what the defining symptoms of surface dyslexia should be. Marshall and Newcombe (1973) had proposed that JC and ST could no longer recognise written words as familiar whole units and had to resort instead to applying their knowledge of the relationship between English letters and sounds to derive a pronunciation of many of the words they saw, though neither JC nor ST was very good at this.

Other surface dyslexics have been shown to possess a better command of what teachers call "phonics" (i.e. the application of letter–sound correspondences). These patients have a reasonable chance of reading a word correctly if that word's spelling matches its pronunciation in a straightforward, regular manner, and so can read words like PINE, CULT and DANCE correctly (because these are words you would probably read correctly even if you had not seen them before). The words that cause problems to surface dyslexics are ones whose spelling and sound are not well matched—the so-called "irregular" or "exception" words of English. Sometimes the divergence between spelling and sound borders on the grotesque, as in words like YACHT ("yott"), QUAY ("kee") and COLONEL ("kernel"). Other, less irregular words contain letters that are pronounced one way in some words and a different way in others. For example, the letters -INT are usually pronounced as in DINT, HINT and MINT but are given a different pronunciation in PINT. A surface dyslexic who is trying to read by the application of spelling-sound correspondences is likely to pronounce PINT so as to rhyme with MINT.

Thus, surface dyslexics read regular words aloud more successfully than irregular words. When faced with an irregular word they often treat it as if it was a regular word, sounding it out in piecemeal fashion; for example, reading COLONEL as "kollonel". Such errors are called *regularisations*. Because Marshall and Newcombe's patients JC and ST were rather poor at applying spelling–sound correspondences, one struggles to find good examples of regularisations in their misreadings.

CLASSIC EXPLANATIONS OF SURFACE DYSLEXIA

Marshall and Newcombe (1973) sought to explain their three forms of acquired dyslexia using a "box and arrow" model of word recognition. Figure 4.1 is not the Marshall and Newcombe model, but is similar, and is typical of the sort of model that was widely used in the 1970s and 1980s (cf. Ellis & Young, 1988; Patterson & Shewell, 1987; Patterson & Morton, 1985; Shallice, 1988), and which remains influential today. Such models characterise the business of reading aloud as involving a number of independent processing components, each of which is dedicated to a different aspect

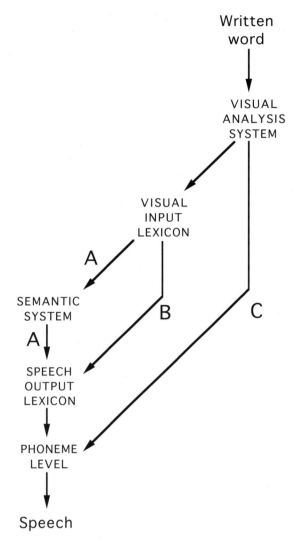

FIG. 4.1   A traditional model of visual word recognition.

of the reading process. We will summarise how such models explain surface dyslexia before going on to discuss more recent, alternative approaches later in the chapter.

Within a model like Fig. 4.1, the job of the *visual analysis system* is to identify the component letters of a word and to code their position in the word. That system should generate the same output for a word like RUBY whether the input is RUBY, ruby, *RUBY* or *ruby*. It is important that letter positions should be coded because RUBY differs from BURY only in the positions of its letters. Damage to the visual analysis system resulting in faulty letter identification and faulty coding of letter positions might be responsible for Marshall and Newcombe's visual dyslexia (Lambon Ralph & Ellis, 1997).

The output of the visual analysis system feeds into the *visual input lexicon*, which contains representations of all the words that a reader has learned to recognise "by sight". Recognising a familiar written word involves activating the appropriate entry in the visual input lexicon. If that happens, then the word on the page conveys a sense of visual familiarity, but the reader does not yet know its meaning. That is because word meanings are stored in the next component, the *semantic system*. Just what the representations of meanings consist of, and whether there is one semantic system or many, are the subjects of much current debate (Saffran & Schwartz, 1994). For the purposes of this chapter we shall assume that there is a single semantic system whose knowledge of rubies (their appearance, use, value, etc.) is activated not only by seeing the written word RUBY, but also by hearing "ruby" or seeing a ruby. But the semantic system does not know the *name* "ruby". The representation that specifies the spoken form of a word is stored in the *speech output lexicon*, a structure that is involved in retrieving spoken words in speech production as well as playing a role in reading. When a spoken word is retrieved from the speech output lexicon, whether in response to semantic input or in response to input from the visual input lexicon, a sequence of consonants and vowels (*phonemes*) is "released" or "activated", which constitutes the word's spoken form. The consonants and vowels are then held at the *phoneme level*, where they may simply be reflected upon (if, for example, you were asked to indicate whether two words rhyme or not) or converted into the instructions required by the articulatory muscles in order to say the word aloud.

One way to read a word aloud, then, is to recognise it as familiar (visual input lexicon), access its meaning (semantic system), then retrieve the corresponding spoken word-form (speech output lexicon). This procedure, which is sometimes called "reading via meaning" or "semantically-mediated reading", is labelled as route A in Fig. 4.1. It is thought by some that deep dyslexics who make semantic errors in reading aloud are reduced to reading via a damaged semantic route A, all other procedures being lost to them (see Plaut & Shallice, 1994). Other patients who have undeniable semantic impairments remain able to read all types of word aloud remarkably well, including irregular words (e.g. Cipolotti & Warrington, 1995; Lambon Ralph, Ellis, & Franklin, 1995; Raymer & Berndt, 1994; Schwartz, Saffran, & Marin, 1980). The existence of such patients has been used to argue for a route from print to sound that operates at the whole-word level but which by-passes the semantic system. One way to create such a route is to propose that direct connections link the corresponding representations of a word in the visual input lexicon and the speech output lexicon—route B in Fig. 4.1. This route could be used to access the pronunciation of a familiar word as soon as it is recognised as familiar by the visual input lexicon. The meaning of the word would not be involved in this process, which could only apply to the reading of words whose written and spoken forms are familiar to the reader.

Routes A and B both rely upon the visual input lexicon recognising a word as familiar, and so can only read words that are already familiar to the reader. They have no ability to read unfamiliar words or invented nonwords such as BEM or KINTEF. Yet normal readers are able to assemble pronunciations for words they have not seen before, or for a psychologist's set of invented nonwords. In models like Fig. 4.1, the procedure for doing this bypasses both the lexicons and the semantic system by taking the products of the visual analysis system (letters coded for position) and translating those letters directly into phonemes. Such a procedure may be termed "non-lexical" because it does not involve the lexicons, "sub-lexical" because translating letters into sounds is presumed to involve units smaller than words (letters and letter groups), or "grapheme–phoneme conversion" because the letters or combinations of letters that correspond to single phonemes (e.g. SH, EA, and TH in SHEATH) are sometimes referred to as "graphemes" (see Coltheart, Curtis, Atkins, & Haller, 1993). This procedure is represented in Fig. 4.1 as route C.

When route C works properly it should generate a correct pronunciation for a nonword or for a word that has a regular spelling. It will, however, treat irregular words as if they were words with regular spelling–sound correspondences, and will therefore regularise them. This, of course, is precisely what surface dyslexics do. Within this framework, then, surface dyslexics are patients who are over-reliant upon route C because of damage to one or more of the components required for the successful functioning of routes A and B. That is, they "sound out" using letter–sound correspondences many words they would previously have been able to read aloud using one or other of the lexical routes (A and B).

DAMAGING THE MODEL

Cognitive neuropsychologists working within this framework assume that injury to the brain can affect each of the components in a model like Fig. 4.1 independently of the others, and can also disrupt the connections between components. Thus, brain injury might damage the visual analysis system but leave the other components intact, or it might selectively damage the connection between the semantic system and speech output lexicon while leaving everything else in working order. Such highly selective impairments might, however, be expected to be rare: the typical stroke or head injury would be expected to affect many components and connections. The challenge for the cognitive neuropsychologist is to devise ways of assessing the status of the different components and connections, to be able to say which continue to work normally and which are damaged in a given patient, and to explain how a different pattern of impaired and intact processes give rise to different patterns of aphasic or dyslexic breakdown.

We have noted that some surface dyslexics remain very good at reading regular words and nonwords, indicating that route C continues to work well for them (e.g. patients HTR of Shallice, Warrington, & McCarthy, 1983, and MP of Bub, Cancelliere, & Kertesz, 1985). In other cases, though, nonword reading is also impaired, suggesting that although the patient relies on route C much of the time, it too is compromised (e.g. Marshall & Newcombe's original surface dyslexics).

It is also worth noting that every surface dyslexic reported to date has managed to read *some* irregular words aloud correctly. If it were possible to block routes A and B completely and force a total reliance on route C, then one might imagine that patients would be found who misread all irregular words, yet that seems not to happen. One possible explanation for this is that psychologists and linguists classify some words as irregular that can actually be read correctly by route C, but that seems unlikely to explain why, for example, patient HTR of Shallice et al. (1983) was able to read correctly such highly irregular words as ANCIENT, ISLE and SIEVE, or why patient NW of Weekes and Coltheart (1996) could read COLONEL, SWORD, and YACHT. Such words seem guaranteed to defy the best efforts of Route C, and the ability of some surface dyslexics to read them correctly leads theorists to concede that most (possibly all) surface dyslexics remain able to read *some* words aloud using the lexical routes A and/or B.

You do not have to spend a great deal of time studying Fig. 4.1 before you realise that damage in more than one place in the model could force a patient to rely more than is normal on route C. If we are clever enough, it should be possible to think of ways to distinguish between the different *subtypes* of surface dyslexia that a model like Fig. 4.1 predicts (see Coltheart & Funnell, 1987; Ellis & Young, 1988; Howard & Franklin, 1987). In this section we shall consider patients who have been held to represent three different varieties of surface dyslexia which we might loosely term "input surface dyslexia", "central (semantic) surface dyslexia", and "output surface dyslexia".

Input surface dyslexia

Damage to the visual input lexicon should, according to Fig. 4.1, block access to routes A and B. Words that were once familiar in written form would now look unfamiliar and the patient would be unable to access their meaning directly from print. If route C was still intact the patient would be able to pronounce regular words correctly, though irregular words would tend to be regularised. If a regular word was successfully converted from print to sound, the patient could then either say the word aloud, or "listen" to its pronunciation internally. If the brain damage had spared the processes responsible for recognising spoken words, and if the semantic system was still intact, the patient should be able to access the meanings of regular words via their sounds. And if the speech output lexicon is also intact, then performance on tasks like picture naming should be preserved.

There is one exception to the claim that patients with "input" surface dyslexia should be able to comprehend regular words correctly via their sounds. Imagine that an input surface dyslexic was asked to read the word HARE and to say what it means. The patient may fail to recognise it as familiar because of damage to the visual input lexicon, but HARE is a regular word, so the patient should be able to generate the correct pronunciation using route C. The patient could then either say the word aloud or listen to it "in his head" and access its meaning via its sound. The problem here is that HARE is a homophone; that is, another word exists which has the same sound but a different meaning (HAIR). The input surface dyslexic will be in danger of pronouncing HARE correctly but then jumping to the wrong interpretation, thinking that the word refers to something that grows on your head (if you're lucky). Coltheart, Masterson, Byng, Prior, and Riddoch (1983) were the first to report and reflect upon such "homophone errors" in surface dyslexia. Examples given by their patients when asked to read and define written words include PANE→"something which hurts" (cf. PAIN) and ROUTE→"what holds the apple tree in the ground and makes it grow" (cf. ROOT).

The same processes that cause an input surface dyslexic to misinterpret homophones will also leave them in danger of misunderstanding irregular words whose regularisations happen to sound like real words. An example is when Marshall and Newcombe's patient JC read LISTEN as "liston" and concluded that the word must be the name of the boxer Sonny Liston. Also, if a nonword happens to sound like a read word (a pseudohomophone like BRANE), then the patient may pronounce it and give it a meaning because it sounds like a word even if it does not look like one.

So have any patients been reported who fit this description? Well, Marshall and Newcombe's (1973) patient JC showed some of the hallmarks. When he was (finally) asked to read sets of regular and irregular words in 1980, JC duly showed a significant regularity effect (Newcombe & Marshall, 1981; 1984). His knowledge of letter–sound correspondences was far from preserved, however, and few of his errors were simple regularisations. He is described as having only slight residual aphasia: Indeed, his spontaneous speech was sufficiently well preserved for him to be proposed for election as a trades union official, a position he was unable to accept because of his reading (and writing) problems. Newcombe and Marshall (1975) state that he had "no difficulty in object naming", though they admit that he showed "occasional word-finding difficulties, especially when nervous" and Newcombe and Marshall (1984) report slight problems naming objects with low frequency names. No data is provided on his comprehension of spoken words. JC appears not to have been given the lexical decision task, but we know that he made errors in homophone comprehension; for example, defining BEE as "to be or not to be, that is the question" and OAR as "that's the ore of metal; the raw materials". And it was JC who defined the irregular word LISTEN as "the boxer".

A second patient who has been proposed as a case of input surface dyslexia is patient EE (Coltheart & Byng, 1989; Howard & Franklin, 1987). EE read regular words better than irregular words and made regularisation errors (e.g. CASTLE→"kastel"; FLOOD→"flude"; SWORD→"swored"). Comprehension of spoken words is reported to have been good (Howard & Franklin, 1987). Homophone misinterpretations were apparent (e.g. DOE→ "something you cook with", BLEW→"colour"). We can find only one example of EE misunderstanding an irregular word because his regularisation error happened to be a word (for him): EE read KNOWS as "kuhNOWs" and added, "one down the Old Kent Road". EE was a Londoner, and in his accent CANAL is pronounced "kuhNOW". In lexical decision, EE falsely accepted many pseudohomophones as being real words while correctly rejecting most ordinary nonwords (Howard & Franklin, 1987). Like JC, however, EE's reading of regular words and nonwords was less than perfectly preserved. EE also had quite severe word-finding problems in speech production (Howard, 1995), which a "pure" case of input surface dyslexia should not.

A third patient who has been reported as matching the requirements of input surface dyslexia is case NW of Weekes and Coltheart (1996). NW read regular words and nonwords aloud almost perfectly, but read only 70% of irregular words correctly, his errors being mostly regularisations (e.g. SUBTLE→"subtul"; QUAY→"kway"). NW is described as showing "no aphasia": he scored 40/40 on a test from the PALPA battery (Kay, Lesser, & Coltheart, 1992), which required him to indicate which of five pictures matches a heard object name. On a separate occasion he named the 40 target pictures from that test correctly. When asked to define the meanings of the same words when they were either spoken to him or presented in written form he defined 37/40 correctly from spoken input compared with 31/40 from written input. When asked to define the 50 difficult and rather obscure words of the National Adult Reading Test (NART; Nelson, 1982) he again did better when they were presented in spoken form (17/50) than when they were presented in written form (5/50). Unfortunately Weekes and Coltheart (1996) provide no control data, so we cannot say for certain that NW's comprehension of spoken words is perfectly normal, but it is clear that he could access word meanings more successfully for spoken words than for written words.

Weekes and Coltheart (1996) do not present any data from standard lexical decision tasks. NW was, however, given a modified lexical decision task in which he was shown two items at a time and was asked to indicate which was the real word. One of the items was always a word with a regular spelling, whereas the other was a pseudohomophone of that word (e.g. GOAT/GOTE; SLEEP/SLEAP). NW was no better than chance on this task (47% correct). He is also reported to have misdefined 4/20 homophones when asked to say what they mean.

In sum, JC and NW probably come closest to the Platonic ideal of a case of "pure" input surface dyslexia. EE had features of input surface dyslexia, but clear signs of output problems too. As well as being candidates for classification as "input surface dyslexics", EE and NW also happen to be two of the very few surface dyslexic patients who have been the subject of documented attempts to remediate their reading. We shall describe those attempts later before presenting our own therapy studies, but must first consider two other proposed sub-types of surface dyslexia.

Central (semantic) surface dyslexia

Some of the first surface dyslexics to be described suffered from progressive dementing illnesses and had profound semantic impairments. For example, patient HTR of Shallice et al. (1983) showed a marked regularity effect and made regularisation errors (e.g. PROVE→"proave", cf. STOVE). Nonword reading was good. She also had profound naming problems (anomia) and poor comprehension of both spoken and written words. Those are the symptoms one would expect to see in a patient with an impaired semantic system. A similar patient, KT, was described by McCarthy and Warrington (1986) and studied further by Patterson and Hodges (1992).

An immediate problem here is that taking out the semantic system alone from Fig. 4.1 should leave a patient with poor naming and poor comprehension but an *intact* ability to read aloud both regular and irregular words using the direct, lexical route B. We have already mentioned the fact that patients have been reported with profound semantic impairments but preserved reading of both regular and irregular words (Cipolotti & Warrington, 1995; Lambon Ralph et al., 1995; Raymer & Berndt, 1994; Schwartz et al., 1980) and that such patients have been interpreted as having damaged semantic systems but intact lexical, non-semantic routes (B).

The semantically impaired surface dyslexics remain able to read *some* highly irregular words aloud correctly. For example, Bub et al.'s (1985) semantically impaired surface dyslexic patient MP remained quite good at reading irregular words that occur frequently in English (e.g. LAUGH, TOUCH), while being much worse at reading irregular words with a lower frequency of occurrence (e.g. SUITE, COUGH). One possibility is that normal readers vary in the efficiency with which route B operates. People in whom route B works well for a wide variety of words will retain good powers of reading aloud even when dementia or some other illness destroys their semantic systems. Other patients whose direct, lexical route only ever worked well for frequently encountered words will, following damage to their semantic systems, have to resort to the sub-lexical route C when trying to read aloud low frequency words. They will become surface dyslexics of the type reported by Bub et al. (1985), McCarthy and Warrington (1986), Shallice et al. (1983), and more recently in a series of papers by Karalyn Patterson, John Hodges, and their colleagues (e.g. Graham, Hodges, & Patterson, 1994; Patterson & Hodges, 1992).

In sum, a substantial number of patients have now been described in whom surface dyslexia co-exists with semantic impairments that affect the comprehension and production of spoken words as well as reading. Fig. 4.1 can only account for these cases if it is proposed that they have limited use of the direct, lexical route B as well as damage to the semantic route C. An alternative account of this form of surface dyslexia, which is especially favoured by Patterson, Hodges and colleagues, will be considered later.

Output surface dyslexia

Looking again at Fig. 4.1, a final way of blocking routes A and B and forcing a reliance upon route C would be to damage the speech output lexicon. Because that lexicon is involved in retrieving spoken words in speaking and naming, tasks such as picture naming will be impaired. In contrast, there need be no impairment of the comprehension of spoken words if the semantic system remains intact.

In fact, if the visual input lexicon and the semantic system are both preserved, then the patient should still be able to recognise written words as familiar *and* access their meanings. What the patient will be unable to do will be to retrieve the spoken form of a written word that has been recognised and understood, because damage to the speech output lexicon will affect the process of accessing spoken word-forms either via semantics (route A) or directly from the visual input lexicon (route B). If the patient is required to read words aloud, he or she will be forced to use route C. That will fail for many irregular words, so the patient should make regularisation errors when trying to read aloud irregular words that he or she should nevertheless show clear signs of understanding. An intact visual input lexicon and semantic system should also make for good lexical decision performance, and there is no reason why homophones should present particular problems.

Patient EST of Kay and Patterson (1985; see also Kay, 1992; Kay & Ellis, 1987) is sometimes held up as a reasonably good example of output surface dyslexia (e.g. Ellis & Young, 1988). EST's speech was anomic and he had problems with picture naming that were not matched by problems in the comprehension of spoken picture names (Kay & Ellis, 1987). His recognition of words in the lexical decision task was much better than his ability to read the same words aloud, though he sometimes failed to accept irregular words as words. However, the trend that EST showed towards better reading of regular than irregular words never attained statistical significance and he made few clear regularisation errors. The errors he made tended instead to be phonological approximations to words of the same sort that he also made when trying to name objects. Also, there are no good examples of EST demonstrating preserved understanding of an irregular word while regularising it. Finally, EST showed evidence of problems in the comprehension of spoken abstract words, implying a degree of semantic impairment in addition to the word-finding problems that undoubtedly contributed to his anomia.

Unlike EST, patient MK of Howard and Franklin (1987) did show a degree of preserved understanding of irregular words, which he nevertheless regularised in reading aloud. For example, shown the word STEAK, he defined it as "nice beef" then immediately read it as "steek". And he did not have any problems with homophones. MK was not, however, especially bad at picture naming, and he showed signs of semantic impairment, particularly affecting the comprehension of abstract words. He was also a "deep dysgraphic", making semantic errors in writing words to dictation and showing better writing of concrete than abstract words.

While most of the patients reported by Patterson, Hodges, and colleagues have had clear semantic deficits, and so fit firmly into the category of central (semantic) surface dyslexia, one of their cases, patient FM, looks more like an output surface dyslexic (Graham et al., 1994; Graham, Patterson, & Hodges, 1995; Patterson & Hodges, 1992). FM's comprehension was only mildly impaired, but she was quite severely anomic as well as being surface dyslexic. She showed effects of frequency in both naming and reading aloud, being better on high than low frequency words in both tasks. In naming, her errors were predominantly semantic, whereas in reading aloud her errors were mostly regularisations. Thus, FM misread many irregular words which she proved capable of responding correctly to in tasks such as choosing which of a set of pictures matches a written object name. The fact that FM showed a mild degree of impairment in comprehension makes her a less-than-pure case of output surface dyslexia, but perhaps the quest for purity can be overdone. FM appears not to have been given lexical decision tasks, so we do not know for sure that she would have classified correctly words she misread, nor that she would have rejected nonwords. Also, FM seems not to have been tested on the comprehension of homophones (which one would not expect to create particular problems).

In sum, the situation with output surface dyslexia is rather like that with input surface dyslexia: No case has yet been reported that matches all the requirements of a pure case, but patients have been reported who come fairly close. There certainly seem to be enough differences between putative input cases such as JC or NW, central semantic cases such as HTR and MP, and an output case such as FM for one to seriously question whether a single explanation will ever account for all of the observed cases of surface dyslexia.

CASE REPORT

We have had the opportunity to study a patient, BS, whose surface dyslexia showed some of the features of the input type, but who was also anomic in a manner more characteristic of output surface dyslexia. We also conducted a study designed to improve his reading and naming.

BS was born in 1962. An intelligent young man, he obtained nine O-levels and four A-levels before embarking on a Chemistry degree. After a year he decided that Chemistry was not for him, and chose instead a 2-year business course. On leaving higher education he worked as manager of a TV rental store, then as marketing manager for a company making rehabilitation aids and equipment. He was in that post when he suffered a cerebral haemorrhage which required a left parietal craniotomy for evacuation of an intra-cerebral haematoma. Assessment at 1 month post-stroke revealed a severe receptive and expressive aphasia together with a loss of vision in his right visual field (a "right homonymous hemianopia"). At 4 months post-stroke, BS was described as being able to follow a simple conversation, and as showing word-finding difficulties in his spontaneous speech, together with occasional jargon output (see Bird & Franklin, 1995–96). He was also reported to have some problems with reading and spelling, and the therapist's notes from that time comment that "Irregularly spelt words are sometimes problematic".

One-and-a-half years after his stroke, BS was living with his parents and receiving weekly speech therapy. He was able to follow conversations well in one-to-one situations, though he complained that he still had problems keeping up with conversations involving greater numbers of participants. His spontaneous speech continued to be slow, with word-finding problems. He had no apparent grammatical or articulatory difficulties, but his reading and spelling remained impaired. His performance on a test of non-verbal intelligence (Raven's progressive matrices) placed him in the top 10% of the population, indicating that his non-verbal intelligence remained intact.

We knew that BS was a surface dyslexic the moment we heard him read COLONEL as "kollonell", but a modern-day assessment requires more than that. BS was given a wide-ranging assessment that explored his comprehension and production of spoken words as well as his reading and spelling. Because BS's improvement was still on-going when we saw him, we will need to bear in mind when some of the different assessments were done. Where control data is referred to, this typically comes from undergraduate students (who we considered to be reasonable controls for a man with BS's background).

Auditory processing

BS's hearing was normal, and he performed well on a range of tests probing the perception and discrimination of speech sounds. In mid-1993 he made more than the normal number of errors on the simple task of repeating heard words, having particular problems with abstract words such as "religion", but by May 1994 he fell (just) within the normal range, repeating 71/80 words correctly after a single taped presentation (test L2 from the ADA battery; Franklin, Turner, & Ellis, 1992).

The auditory lexical decision task is like the visual lexical decision task except that this time the patient listens to a random sequence of spoken words and nonwords and indicates whether each one was a word or not. BS made a few more errors than normal controls when first tested in mid-1993, showing a tendency to reject abstract words as not being words, but he was once again within the normal range by early 1994 (words 77/80; nonwords 76/80 on ADA test L1).

BS's ability to match spoken picture names to the corresponding pictures was good (64/66 with 2 self-corrections on ADA test S2 in April 1994), as was his performance (50/52 correct) on the version of the Pyramids and Palm Trees test (Howard & Patterson, 1992) in which the patient must select which of two pictures "goes with" a word spoken by the examiner (for example, choosing the picture of a dog rather than a cat when the examiner says "kennel").

The ADA synonym matching task (S1) requires the patient to listen to pairs of spoken words and decide if the words in each pair are similar or different in meaning. The pairs include abstract words (e.g. similar: "command, order"; different: "fraud, toil") as well as concrete words (e.g. similar: "basin, bowl"; different: "pot, ship"). BS scored 135/160 in mid-1993, which is outside the normal range for young adults (152–160). At that time his problems particularly affected abstract and low frequency words. He had improved to 148/160 by January 1994, and by November 1994, was again at the bottom end of the normal range (152/160).

Object recognition and naming

BS's ability to remember the names of objects was impaired throughout the time we were involved in assessing and treating him, though like his spoken word recognition it showed gradual improvement. For example, in mid-1993 BS could name only 28 of a set of 66 black-and-white line drawings of familiar objects correctly, but by April 1994 he named 47/66. In April/May 1994 BS named 30/40 objects on the naming test from the PALPA battery (Kay et al., 1992) and 8/15 of the objects from the short naming test of the Birmingham Object Recognition battery (BORB; Riddoch & Humphreys, 1992). Both scores are well below the normal range.

BS was not tested in the early days on his ability to recognise objects for what they are (as distinct from naming them). However, in January 1994 he scored 48/52 on a different version of the Pyramids and Palm Trees test—this time one in which the patient is shown three pictures and must indicate which of the two below "goes with" the one on top (e.g. matching a picture of a kennel to a dog rather than a cat). This is just one more error than normal controls are said to make. And in April 1994 he made no errors at all on a similar task ("associative matching" from the BORB). Thus, BS showed a good ability to recognise and access stored knowledge about objects at a time when he was still having great difficulty naming them.

We wanted to find a set of pictures that BS had fairly consistent difficulty naming in order to use them later in therapy. One hundred and thirty-nine pictures of objects were presented on three separate occasions in May 1994 for naming. These were taken from a set of black-and-white line drawings published by Snodgrass and Vanderwart (1980). BS named 91 pictures correctly on the first and second occasions, and 80 on the third occasion. Sometimes when he tried to recall the name of an object it refused to come (e.g. IRON→"One I never get right"; BRUSH→"I know what that one is. For your hair. No"), sometimes he would define the object in an effort to show that he knew what it was (e.g. OSTRICH→"Type of a bird"; SCALES→"Some type of a weight"). On other occasions he produced the name of a related object (e.g. SLIDE→"swing"; WHALE→"seal"). Such "semantic errors" were often rejected as he made them (e.g. GIRAFFE→"zebra, no it's not"; KING→"Not a queen") or self-corrected (e.g. NUN→"convent, er, nun"; CHAIN→"link, er, chain"). Across a range of different sets of items, errors where he failed to respond to a picture or just said "No" accounted for 38% of BS's naming errors, definitions for 11% and semantic errors for 57%. Only a few phonological errors (3%) were observed (e.g. CRAB→"grab"; CATERPILLAR→"catterbittle").

There was some consistency across testing sessions in which items he could name and which he could not. Thus, he named 53 (38%) of the 139 pictures correctly on all three occasions, whereas he failed to name 16 pictures (12%) on any occasion. There were, however, 35 (25%) pictures which he named correctly twice but failed to remember the name of on the third occasion, and another 35 (25%) which he named only once and forgot the names of twice. To give a specific example, BS failed to remember the word "cloud" in the first and third sessions but remembered it in the second session. This suggests that the word "cloud" was in his vocabulary (speech output lexicon) all along, but that it resisted his efforts to access it on the first and third attempts. The same conclusion is indicated by the fact that BS was often able to recall a word once given its initial sound or sounds as a cue. Although we did not assess the effects of cueing formally, when he was struggling to name a picture we would usually end the trial by giving him a cue, which rarely failed to elicit the name (e.g. SHELL→"... [Experimenter: "sh"] shell"; CACTUS→"Difficult one ... [Experimenter: "ca"] cactus").

Several lines of evidence pointed to BS's naming problems being due to difficulties in retrieving spoken word-forms from the speech output lexicon. Thus, he continued to have difficulty naming objects at a time when he performed well on tasks that require objects to be recognised and understood but not named, and well on matching spoken object names to pictures. Many of his errors were omissions or attempts to show that he knew what objects were when he could not name them. We would interpret his semantic errors, which he often rejected spontaneously, as a by-product of this prolonged search for names (cf. Caramazza & Hillis, 1990). BS's inconsistency in naming, and the ability of phonemic cues to trigger correct naming, suggested to us that the names he failed to retrieve unaided were in his speech output lexicon throughout and that his problems lay in accessing them. In other words, the source of the naming deficit seemed to lie along the arrow connecting the semantic system to the speech output lexicon.

Reading

BS continued to have difficulty with reading as well as naming. He had no problems recognising, matching, and naming single letters, scoring 26/26 on naming letters and matching upper- to lower-case letters, but his reading aloud showed the characteristics of surface dyslexia. In July 1993 BS was asked to read aloud the regular and irregular words of test 35 from the PALPA battery. He read 25/30 regular words, correctly but only 12/30 irregular words, which represents a significant advantage for the regular words, $\chi^2 = 11.92$, $df = 1$, $P < .01$. His errors included the regularisations COLONEL→"kollonell", BREAK → "breek", SWORD → "swored", and PINT read to rhyme with MINT.

By January 1994 BS was able to read 29/30 regular and 23/30 irregular words from PALPA test 35. There is still a trend towards better reading of regular than irregular words, but there is also a clear improvement on his reading of the same words 6 months earlier, McNemar $\chi^2 = 11.53$, $df = 1$, $P < .01$. Further word sets were presented for reading aloud between February 1994 and January 1995. The results are shown in Table 4.1. What is clear is that by this time BS's problems in reading aloud mainly affected words that were not only irregular in their spelling–sound correspondences but were also of low frequency and/or abstract in meaning—words like TEAK and TROUGH (which are low frequency), or UNIQUE and SCARCE (which are abstract).

We wanted to assemble a list of words that BS had consistent difficulty reading aloud for use in therapy. Two hundred irregular words were culled from a variety of published sources and given to BS on three separate occasions in May 1994. He read 123 (62%) correctly on the first occasion, 143 (72%) on the second occasion, and 152 (76%) on the third occasion. He read 100 of the 200 words correctly on all three occasions (50%) and failed to read 28 words correctly on any occasion (14%). There were an additional 46 (23%) that he read correctly twice but misread once, and 26 (13%) that he read correctly only once. Sixty-five per cent of the errors BS made across the three administrations of these words could be classed as regularisations: the remaining paralexias were mostly visual errors (20%) in which the error

TABLE 4.1

BS's performance on tests of reading aloud regular and irregular words varying on frequency and imageability

Source of materials (and date of test)		Word types		
Patterson & Hodges (1992) (April 1994)		Regular		Exceptional (irregular)
	High frequency	38/42		34/42
	Low frequency	40/42		26/42
Seidenberg, Waters, Barnes, & Tanenhaus (1984) (May 1994)		Regular consistent	Regular inconsistent	Strange (very irregular)
	High frequency	12/15	15/15	11/15
	Low frequency	13/15	12/15	9/15
Strain, Patterson, & Seidenberg (1994) (January 1995)		Regular		Exceptional (irregular)
	High imageability	15/16		13/16
	Low imageability	13/16		7/16

was a real word which shared at least half its letters in common with the target word (e.g. CHAOS→"choose"; SPATIAL→"spatula").

Test 39 from the PALPA battery requires the patient to read and define a list of 20 words, half of which are regular and half irregular, and all of which are homophones. In September 1993 BS read 10/10 regular words correctly and 7/10 irregular words, while in January 1994 he read 10/10 regular words and 6/10 irregular words. On both occasions there were clear examples of homophone errors in definition, e.g. MAIL→"this is a man" (cf. MALE); PROPHET→"this is earning money, maybe" (cf. PROFIT); WEEK→"soft, becomes bent" (cf. WEAK); HAUL→"something in a house" (cf. HALL); PALE→"keep water in" (cf. PAIL); PAIN→"could be a window" (cf. PANE). In the same test he read GREAT as "greet" (a regularisation error) and added, "hold with somebody . . . show them around".

We know that BS had word retrieval problems. One might therefore have been tempted to regard his surface dyslexia as of the "output" type in which damage to the speech output lexicon blocks both the lexical reading routes and forces the use of the sub-lexical route C to read aloud. But we have argued that such patients should not have problems understanding homophones and should show some understanding of the meanings of exception words they fail to read correctly. BS did not do that: He often misunderstood homophones and words whose regularisations happen to be another word. And in many sessions of testing he never showed any indication of understanding the meaning of an irregular word he could not read aloud correctly.

Those observations, plus BS's good auditory comprehension, lead us to believe that although he had undoubted speech output problems, his surface dyslexia bore hallmarks of the input type. If this were the correct diagnosis, then when BS was asked to discriminate words from nonwords in the lexical decision task he should tend to reject some words and falsely accept nonwords which, when pronounced, sound like real words ("pseudohomophones" like BRITE and BRUME). In April 1994 BS was given lexical decision test 27 from the PALPA battery. The real words in this test are half regular words and half irregular words, whereas the nonwords are half pseudohomophones and half ordinary nonwords. BS accepted 14/15 regular words and 13/15 irregular words as words, failing (like EE before him) to show the predicted problems with irregular words. He did, however, mistakenly accept 9 out of 15 pseudohomophones as words, while correctly rejecting all 15 of the ordinary (non-homophonic) nonwords.

One might expect a patient who made so many regularisations to be good at reading nonwords. BS was not very bad at this, but not fully normal either: his performance (16/20) on a set of graded nonwords (Snowling, Stothard, & McLean, 1996) put him within the range of normal 9–11 year olds, and his reading of the nonwords from PALPA test 36 showed that he had particular problems with longer nonwords (three-letter, 6/6; four-letter, 6/6; five-letter, 5/6; six-letter, 3/6). Thus, although BS's capacity for letter–sound conversion (route C in Fig. 4.1) was reasonably good, it was probably not fully normal.

THERAPY STUDY

With a case like BS it would be possible to go on assessing and reassessing virtually forever, progressively refining your understanding of just what had gone wrong with his speech and language. But BS was a young man keen to reacquire his language skills, and we were keen to help him if we could. We set out, therefore, to try and improve his reading and naming.

We wanted our therapy study to satisfy a number of other requirements. First among these was that the treatments we attempted should be grounded in the understanding we had developed of his problems. Cognitive neuropsychologists debate the extent to which treatment recommendations can be derived from their assessments. Some are fairly pessimistic (e.g. Caramazza 1989; Hillis, 1993), whereas others, including ourselves, are more optimistic (e.g. Behrmann & Byng, 1992; Crerar, Ellis, & Dean, 1996). We felt that the provisional conclusions we had reached suggested at the very least that some procedures might be more successful than others at restoring his reading and naming.

A second requirement was that changes observed over the treatment period should unambiguously reflect the effects of treatment programme and should not be attributable to the slow, spontaneous improvement that was undoubtedly taking place. A third consideration was that any improvements should be demonstrably due to the specific therapy given rather than to any more general increase in BS's motivation and efforts to help himself resulting from the fact that he was receiving individual attention from people eager to help him (sometimes referred to as "charm effects").

Fourth on our list of requirements was that the treatments should be practical and reasonable procedures that other therapists could adapt and use with patients of their own. Some of the published therapy studies in cognitive neuropsychology have involved treatments so time-consuming and of such intensity that no therapist working in a normal clinical setting could hope to emulate them. We sought to create treatments that were not too time-consuming, and which BS could work at on his own, or with the help of a family member.

Finally, we wanted to know if any benefits of treatment would be maintained once the treatment stopped. One would not be inclined to recommend treatments whose benefits are short-lived, whereas treatments whose effects are sustained and long-lasting are treatments that others may wish to invest time and effort in.

Our study was informed by the previous work of Byng and Coltheart (1986) and Coltheart and Byng (1989) who succeeded in improving the reading of patient EE, who we discussed earlier as a possible case of "input surface dyslexia". They taught EE to read correctly words he had previously misread by pairing each word with a picture to give some indication of the word's meaning (for example, the card for the word BOROUGH had a small map of part of London on it, and the card for BOUGH showed a drawing of a tree). EE showed substantial improvement on the words treated in this way, but he also improved to a lesser extent on words which were *not* treated. Coltheart and Byng concluded that their therapy was capable of restoring the representations of treated words in the visual input lexicon to a level where they could sustain error-free reading, but that in so doing they also improved the functioning of that lexicon more generally. A similar therapy study, published after we did our study with BS, was carried out by Weekes and Coltheart (1996) on patient NW.

We used an approach called a "cross-over treatment design", which has been developed to address some of these issues and which, when successful, establishes beyond reasonable doubt that any observed improvements in the patient's performance are a result of the treatment, and not spontaneous improvement or charm effects (Coltheart, 1983; Crerar et al., 1996). The design can be used when the patient has at least two impairments that can be worked upon one after the other. BS's problems in naming and reading, which we thought to arise from impairments around the speech output lexicon and the visual input lexicon respectively, seemed to fit the bill.

BS's results on the three administrations of the 139-picture naming task and the 200-word reading task were used to derive a set of pictures that he had clear difficulty naming and a set of words that he had clear difficulty reading. Both sets were divided in half to create one set of pictures and another set of words that would be worked on during the treatment programme and one set of each that would not be involved in treatment but would be assessed before and after.

The three presentations of both the 139 pictures and the 200 words happened in May 1994. Fifty-two pictures were selected which he had failed to name on two ($n=35$) or three ($n=17$) occasions. These were divided into two sets of 26, which were matched in terms of BS's ability to name them. Similarly, 52 words were selected which BS had failed to read on two ($n=24$) or three ($n=28$) occasions. These were divided into two sets of 26, which were matched in terms of his ability to read them.

Performance on all 52 pictures and 52 words was assessed on 6 June 1994. There then followed a period of three weeks during which BS worked at relearning the names of the 26 treated pictures. All the words and pictures were assessed for a second time on 27 June 1994. Therapy then switched to teaching BS to re-read the 26 treated words. We had intended to continue the therapy for three weeks (the same time as for the naming therapy), but after two weeks BS insisted that he had learned the words and did not want to spend another week working through lists he said he could already read. We therefore conducted the third full assessment on 11 July 1994. BS was then left alone for 11 weeks, at the end of which a fourth and final assessment was carried out on 29 September 1994.

The naming therapy

We believed that BS was having difficulty retrieving spoken word-forms from his speech output lexicon, both in spontaneous speech and in picture naming. Two other things we knew about him were that he responded well to initial phoneme cues and that his letter–sound conversion was reasonably good. Our naming therapy was based on this knowledge.

BS was given two booklets to work with. The booklets contained four pages for each of the 26 treated items. The first page for a given item had just a picture of the object to be named. BS was asked to try to name it from the picture alone. If he could not, he turned to the next page, which had the picture and, underneath it, the first letter which, for the items chosen, corresponded to the first sound of the object's name. BS tried again to name the picture, this time with the help of the (self-generated) initial phoneme cue. If still unsuccessful, he turned to the third page, which had the picture plus the first half (approximately) of the written name, providing a more substantial cue. He tried again. The fourth picture had the picture plus the full written name on it. If BS felt that he had managed to name the picture when looking at one of the earlier sheets he was instructed to turn to the fourth page to check that he was right.

We suggested to BS that he should spend about 20 minutes a day on this task, and that he should alternate between the two booklets. We felt that 13 items per session was enough for BS to work on, and alternating the books ensured a roughly equal amount of attention to each item. BS worked largely on his own for the next 3 weeks, our involvement being limited to short, weekly visits to check that he was persisting with the task and that everything was going well. Because he worked alone, we do not have data on the precise amount of time spent, or on such niceties as how far through the sets of four pages he needed to progress before accessing the correct name for each item. It is necessary to relinquish a degree of experimental control when devising tasks that patients can work at on their own, but we felt that such a sacrifice was worthwhile in the cause of creating a practical and adaptable treatment.

The reading therapy

We believed that BS's surface dyslexia was caused by problems in accessing the representations of written words in the visual input lexicon. Coltheart and Byng (1989) had reported some success with a similar patient, EE, using a task in which written words were paired with pictures which suggested the word's meaning. Some of our therapy words were hard to picture (e.g. SPATIAL, ROUTINE, ALLEGE), and we felt that a simpler procedure would serve to enable BS to reassociate these written words with their meanings and pronunciations. By the time this study was done, BS's comprehension of spoken words had returned to normal levels, and we believed that if BS saw a difficult word and heard it at the same time, the spoken word would activate its meaning and provide its pronunciation, and that the simultaneous presence of written word, spoken word, and meaning would help the links between the three to be re-established.

The reading therapy was very simple, and was something BS could work at on his own. He was given four sheets of paper, each of which had the 26 treated words printed on it in capital letters in a single column. The words were typed in a different order on each sheet. Rather like a foreign language course, each sheet was accompanied by a different audio cassette on which the 26 words had been recorded in the appropriate order. BS began a session by selecting a sheet and its accompanying tape. He was instructed to look at the first word on the list and try to read it. He then played the first section of tape and heard the word being spoken. If he had read it correctly he was told to move on to the next word. If he had misread it he was to look hard at the word, repeat its correct pronunciation to himself several times, and think about its meaning. This continued to the end of the list. The idea of using four different orders was to avoid BS simply learning by rote the order in which the words occurred. He was asked to choose a different list each day and to spend about 20 minutes per day on the therapy.

Once again we limited ourselves to short, weekly visits to check on compliance and progress. As noted previously, we had intended to continue the therapy for 3 weeks (the same time as for the naming therapy), but after 2 weeks BS told us that he had learned the words and did not want to spend another week on them. We therefore conducted the third full assessment.

Results

The results of the therapy study are shown in Fig. 4.2. The four lines on that graph show the number correct out of 26 for BS naming the treated and untreated pictures, and reading the treated and untreated words.

At the outset (Assessment 1) BS was a little better at naming the pictures than reading the words, but there was no difference in either case between treated and untreated sets (because they had been carefully matched, and the treatments had yet to begin). Between the first and second assessments BS worked at learning to name the 26 pictures in the treated set. We can see that at Assessment 2, 3 weeks later, his performance on the treated picture

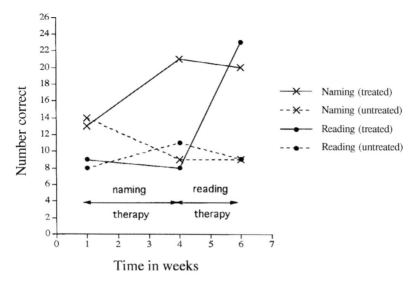

FIG. 4.2   Effects of naming and reading therapy on the ability of patient BS to name treated and untreated pictures and to read treated and untreated irregular words.

set had improved from 13/26 before therapy to 21/26 after therapy. This differ-ence is statistically significant, McNemar $\chi^2 = 4.08$, $df = 1$, $P < .05$. It is also clear from Fig. 4.2 that improvement between the first and second assessments was limited to the treated picture set: Performance on the untreated set showed a slight, though non-significant, decline, and reading accuracy remained unchanged for both word sets.

Between Assessments 2 and 3, 2 weeks later, BS switched to the reading therapy. We can see that over this period there was a dramatic improvement in his ability to read the treated set of words—from 8/26 at Assessment 2 to 23/26 at Assessment 3, McNemar $\chi^2 = 13.07$, $df = 1$, $P < .01$. Although he had not worked on the treated picture set between Assessments 2 and 3, performance on that set was maintained. In contrast, no change in perfor-mance was detectable for the untreated words or the untreated pictures.

Thus, BS showed improvements in picture naming as a result of the naming therapy, and improvement in reading as a result of the reading therapy, but in both cases the benefits were confined to the treated items. There was no generalisation to untreated items, implying that any spoken word that BS wished to reacquire, or any written word he wanted to learn to read again, would have to be worked on individually. This pattern of results confirmed that the improvements were indeed due to the therapy itself and not to spontaneous improvement or a general charm effect, both of which would be expected to lead to some improvement on untreated items.

BS's naming and reading held up well over the 11-week rest period. At the end of September 1994 he named 18/26 treated pictures correctly but only 9/26 untreated pictures, and he read 22/26 treated written words correctly but only 13/26 untreated words. We were obviously delighted that the gains in reading and naming survived an interval approaching 3 months in length.

We interpret the results of the therapy study as showing that practice at naming pictures improved the ability of the semantic representations of those items to access the corresponding spoken word-forms in the speech output lexicon without improving access to the lexicon generally. We never established as clearly whether BS's problems in visual word recognition were due to damage within the visual input lexicon itself or damage to the connections between the visual input lexicon and the semantic system. If the former, we would say that the reading therapy restored the representations of words in that lexicon without improving the functioning of that lexicon more generally; if the latter, we would say that the reading therapy improved the ability of representations in the visual input lexicon to access the corresponding representation of word meanings in the semantic system without improving those connections more generally. We do not have an explanation of why EE and NW showed generalisation to untreated items whereas BS did not.

CONNECTIONISM, SURFACE DYSLEXIA, AND THE "TRIANGLE MODEL"

All of the theorising thus far has involved the use of functional models of the sort that Marshall and Newcombe (1973) would have felt entirely at home with. The time has come, however, to acknowledge an alternative framework for thinking about word recognition and reading, which has been gathering momentum over a number of years, and whose most recent instantiation is a major paper by Plaut, McClelland, Seidenberg, and Patterson (1996). That paper is very technical in places, and a more reader-friendly exposition that focuses particularly on the application of the approach to surface dyslexia has been provided by Patterson et al. (1997; see also Plaut, 1997).

The alternative theoretical framework is set out in Fig. 4.3. That figure represents a *connectionist* or *distributed processing* model of reading, elements of which have been brought into being in the form of a computer model which is designed to "simulate" some aspects of normal reading. All connectionist models have in common the fact that they are built up from simple processing units which are grouped into pools representing aspects of spelling, meaning, or pronunciation. Thus, in the computer model the pool of units labelled "Orthography" consists of units representing either individual letters such as B, M, or I or frequently occurring combinations of letters such as TH-, -EE-, and -CH. The pool labelled "Phonology" contains units

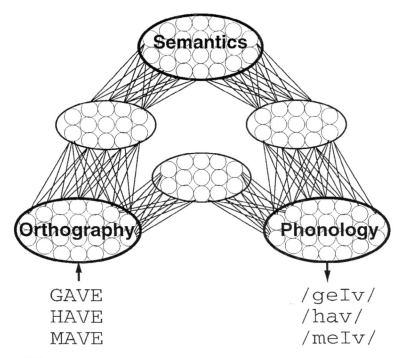

FIG. 4.3 The triangle model (reproduced wth permission from Plaut, 1997).

that represent individual consonants and vowels. The computer model can only deal with one-syllable words, and the units for different sounds are coded for where they occur in their syllable. Thus, there is one unit in the phonological pool for "b" in the beginning of a syllable and another unit for "b" at the end.

All the units in a pool are connected to all the units in the other pools via what are called "hidden units" (the blank ellipses in Fig. 4.3 whose role will be mentioned shortly). When the model is first set up, all of the connections are effectively of equal strength. Thus, the strength of the connections linking the orthographic unit for the letter B to the phonological unit for the sound "b" is no stronger at the outset than the strength of the connections between B and "m" or B and "z". Teaching the model to read consists of activating the orthographic and phonological units for different words, and having the model gradually adjust the strengths of connections until the useful ones are strong and the less useful ones are weak. Thus, the connections involved in getting from B to "b" and M to "m" would be strengthened, while those involved in getting from B to "m" and M to "b" would be weakened.

The so-called "hidden units" play an important role in this learning process. When the model is first set up, they do not represent anything at all, but as the training proceeds they gradually detect higher-order relationships such as the fact that whereas the letters I, N, and T should activate the phonological unit for the short vowel "i" when preceded by D ("dint"), H ("hint"), or M ("mint"), a different vowel unit needs to be activated when HINT is preceded by P ("pint"). Hence, hidden units are important for capturing the regularities on which generalisation is based, and also for allowing the model to read irregular words correctly.

In connectionist models of this sort no distinction is made between levels at which letters or phonemes are represented and levels at which words are represented. That is, there are no lexical units representing individual words, and no lexicons in which only word units are stored. Instead, a word is a pattern of activity over a set of orthographic units (its spelling), phonological units (its sound), and semantic units (its meaning). That is why these models are said to employ "distributed" representations. And the fact that much of the knowledge that a trained model possesses is embodied in the strength of its connections leads them to be called "connectionist" models.

Figure 4.3 shows three pools of units, hence the framework is referred to as the "triangle model". But although some connectionist models have implemented something akin to semantic units representing elements of word meanings (see Plaut & Shallice, 1994), the present simulation of the triangle model only maps letter strings (orthographic units) onto sounds (phonological units). There are no semantic units yet implemented in the triangle model.

After training, the triangle model can generate the correct pronunciations of virtually all of the words on which it has been trained (and it has a "vocabulary" of several thousand one-syllable words). That is, for example, if the programmer switches on the orthographic units for SH, EE, and P the model will generate the pronunciation "sheep". More than that, if the programmer types in a string of letters that is not in its training vocabulary (e.g. a nonword like SHOOP), the model makes as good a stab at pronouncing it as human readers do. This is because, having learned to associate SH with "sh", OO with "oo", and P with "p" through training on words like SHIP, SHOOT and LOOP, the model can translate SH + OO + P into sound quite effectively. It does this using exactly the same knowledge (connections) that it uses to read SHIP, SHOOT, LOOP, and many other real words. That is, there is no distinction in the triangle model between lexical and non-lexical reading routes.

In the recent simulations, the model receives different amounts of training on different words. In fact, training is in proportion to the frequency with which different words occur in English. This means that the model is taught the relationship between the spelling and the sound of high frequency words like MEET and

FOOT more often than it is taught the relationship between the spelling and the sound of low frequency words such as LUSH and DEAF. When the model is trained in this way, associations between spelling and sound only develop efficiently for higher frequency words. Despite this fact, the model learns to pronounce regular low frequency words such as LUSH correctly because the connections involved in converting L + U + SH into "lush" are also involved in reading other words such as LUCK, LASH, and GUSH.[1]

When the amount of training on a word reflects its frequency, then the connections required to read a low frequency, irregular ("exception") word such as DEAF may not be very strong, and can struggle to compete with the connections developed to read regular words such as DEAN, MEAT and LEAF. This means that such low frequency, irregular words will be vulnerable to any damage to the network which will show a tendency to read DEAF as "deef"; that is, to a tendency to regularise low frequency, irregular words. Just like surface dyslexics do.

So how do proponents of the triangle model propose that normal readers normally manage to avoid regularising low frequency irregular words? Triangular theorists believe that we are able to read low frequency exception words correctly because of some support from the semantic route (orthographic units→semantic units→phonological units). We noted earlier that the computer model does not include genuine semantic units: The notion of a semantic contribution to reading aloud has only been implemented using a token additional source of input to the phonological units. That additional input, which is meant to mimic what would happen if there was a genuine semantic contribution, pushes the phonological units in the direction of the correct pronunciation. In so doing, it helps low frequency, irregular words to overcome the tendency the model would otherwise have to regularise them.

Once the model has been trained with the additional "semantic" support in place, that support can be switched off. When that is done, the model once again shows a pattern remarkably like that of surface dyslexics—it reads high frequency words well, whether regular or irregular, and also reads low frequency regular words well, but it regularises some low frequency, irregular words.

We have, then, a theory of human surface dyslexia embodied in a working computer simulation. The theory proposes that the semantic route from print to sound plays a role in normal reading aloud, and is especially needed for the accurate reading of low frequency, irregular words. Brain damage that affects that route leaves the reader more reliant on direct conversion of orthography to phonology and reveals the intrinsic problems that the direct route has with low frequency, irregular words.

---

[1] How well this works depends on your accent.

SUB-TYPES WITHIN THE TRIANGLE MODEL?

When we considered traditional models of word recognition such as Fig. 4.1, we realised that those models predict that surface dyslexia might arise from damage at more than one location in the model, resulting in different sub-types of surface dyslexia. We would argue that the same is true for the triangle model. Specifically, we would argue that the triangle model predicts the existence of distinct "input", "central" and "output" forms of surface dyslexia, just as the old-style models do.

Central (semantic) surface dyslexia

Within the triangle model, anything that reduces the contribution of the semantic route to reading aloud will tend to induce surface dyslexia. One way to reduce the contribution of the semantic route would be to damage the semantic system itself. This is what is thought to happen in the patients with what we earlier called "central (semantic) surface dyslexia".[2] These patients have progressive dementing illnesses, which means that over time they gradually lose more and more of their understanding of the meanings of objects and words. As Patterson et al. (1997) observe, three studies have now been published which show that patients with these progressive disorders remain able to read correctly irregular words which they still understand, but once their understanding of the meaning of a word goes, they start to regularise it in reading aloud (Funnell, 1996; Graham et al., 1994; Hillis & Caramazza, 1991). That is, irregular words can still be read correctly while their semantic representations remain viable, but once those semantic representations have degraded to the point where they no longer sustain comprehension, then reading aloud is mediated purely by the connections between pools of orthographic and phonological units, connections that are inherently prone to regularise (lower frequency) irregular words.

Funnell (1996) showed that her patient, EP, could still read most irregular words correctly as long as she retained some inkling of what they meant. EP's comprehension did not have to be precise in order to support correct reading. EP was able to read irregular object names correctly at a time when she could no longer reliably choose between the corresponding object picture and the picture of a related object. For example, she read VASE correctly when she could no longer choose reliably between a picture of a vase and a picture of a jug in a written word-to-picture matching task. EP could, however, choose the picture of the vase reliably when the alternative

---

[2] Note that for these cases there is no need to invoke additional damage to a direct, lexical route (B in Fig. 4.1). The merging of lexical and non-lexical processes in distributed processing models means that the capabilities assigned to routes B and A in Fig. 4.1 are the property of the single set of connections between orthographic and phonological units in Fig. 4.3.

was a picture of an unrelated object (a kangaroo). Funnell suggested that for irregular words the semantic route generates a spoken response that is different from the response generated by a sub-lexical reading route (which, in Funnell's formulation, is more like route C of Fig. 4.1 than the orthography to phonology mapping of the triangle model). When the word conveys some meaning to the patient, Funnell argues, then the semantically mediated pronunciation will be selected; but when the word conveys no meaning, then reading is mediated by the sub-lexical route, resulting in the regularisation of irregular words.

Output surface dyslexia

Returning to the triangle model, dissolution of the semantic system is not the only possible cause of surface dyslexia within that model. Weakening the connections between an intact semantic system and phonological units could achieve the same result. Such a (partial) disconnection could go some way towards explaining "output surface dyslexics" whose comprehension of spoken words is reasonably good but who are both anomic and surface dyslexic. Indeed, this is the explanation offered by Patterson et al. (1997) for patient FM whose comprehension was only mildly impaired, but who was quite severely anomic as well as surface dyslexic (Graham et al., 1994, 1995).

An association has been demonstrated in central, semantic surface dyslexia between comprehension and the tendency to regularise irregular words. In output surface dyslexia, one would predict an association between naming and reading. If a patient can no longer name an object (or concept), then the written name of that thing should tend to be regularised in reading aloud if it has an irregular spelling. This should occur even if the patient can still demonstrate an understanding of the word's meaning in tasks involving comprehension of pictures or spoken word.

As far as we are aware, this prediction has not been tested for "ordinary" output surface dyslexics. It has been shown to hold, however, for a patient who could understand both concrete and abstract words when they were presented in written form, but who had problems retrieving abstract words in speech production. Patient DRB was as good as normal controls when it came to generating spoken exemplars of semantic categories containing imageable items (e.g. animals or colours), but was poor at generating spoken exemplars of semantic categories containing more abstract items (e.g. religions or emotions). He demonstrated good understanding of written abstract words, but was bad at reading aloud those with irregular spellings (Franklin, Howard, & Patterson, 1995). Within the triangle model, the explanation of this pattern could be that DRB's semantic representations of abstract words were preserved, but that he was impaired when it came to using those semantic representations to activate phonological representations (Franklin et al., 1995). That is, lack of semantic support for the reading of abstract words made DRB surface dyslexic for such words. In contrast, he was not surface dyslexic for concrete words because he was not anomic for those words either.

Input surface dyslexia?

It seems to us that the triangle model quite clearly predicts the existence of a third, input form of surface dyslexia, though it has not been discussed thus far in accounts of the model. Damage to the links between orthography and semantics would leave the semantic representations intact, and would not cause the patient to become anomic, but *would* reduce the ability of the semantic route to contribute to reading aloud. Hence, damage to the links between orthography and semantics should cause a patient to become surface dyslexic, and the surface dyslexia would be an "input" type.

We would suggest that damage of that nature was responsible for at least some of the aspects of BS's surface dyslexia. BS was not semantically impaired at a time when he remained a surface dyslexic: by mid-1994 he was performing within the normal range for undergraduate students on tasks assessing the comprehension of spoken words, both concrete and abstract, and he scored at normal levels on tasks assessing knowledge of pictured objects. He was still anomic, however, when he was also surface dyslexic. Our analysis of his naming problems suggested that they lay more in accessing phonological representations than in any damage to the representations themselves. Thus, a problem in transmission of activation between the semantic system and phonology seems to have been a component of his overall pattern.

There are, however, features of BS's reading that do not readily fit the pattern expected of output surface dyslexia. The first relates to the visual errors that constituted some 20% of BS's reading errors. If BS's orthographic system and semantic system were intact, and the links from orthography to semantics were also intact, why would he read CHAOS as "choose" or SPATIAL as "spatula"? Plaut and Shallice (1994) developed a connectionist model of reading via meaning in which orthographic units connected to semantic units and thence to phonological units. They then showed that apparent "visual" errors could occur even when the connections between semantic and phonological units were damaged. We cannot, therefore, rule out *a priori* the possibility that BS's visual errors were a by-product of damage to the connection between his semantic and phonological systems. However, in Plaut and Shallice's model, the proportion of visual errors made following damage to the model was much greater for lesions near the orthographic units than for more remote lesions. Also, when the triangle model was trained with token semantic input to the phonological units, and that input was then withdrawn making the model surface dyslexic, Patterson et al. (1997) observe that "Essentially all of the errors were regularisations." That is, there were few or no visual errors. So visual errors are *not* an inevitable consequence of damage to any part of a connectionist reading system, and do not arise within the current triangle model when it is transformed into an output surface dyslexic by loss of the input to phonology from semantics.

We would also note that some surface dyslexics have been reported who make few or no visual errors, only regularisation errors. Patterson et al. (1997) call these the "purest cases of reported human surface dyslexia". They include central, semantic surface dyslexics such as MP (Behrmann & Bub, 1992; Bub et al., 1985) and KT (McCarthy & Warrington, 1986; Patterson & Hodges, 1992). If lesioning the semantic system does not cause significant numbers of visual errors, either in people or in the triangle model, it is not clear how damage to the links from semantics to phonology of the sort probably responsible for BS's anomia could also be held responsible for his visual errors.

Another problem we have with explaining BS's surface dyslexia solely in terms of impaired links from semantics to phonology is that we cannot see how such a lesion could cause a patient to make homophone confusions. If BS's orthographic system, his semantic system, and the links between the two were all working normally, why did he look at HAUL and say "something in a house", or look at PROPHET and say "this is earning money, maybe"? The orthography to semantics links, if intact, should have activated the correct meanings of those words and blocked such errors. They should also have prevented him from misinterpreting the meaning of irregular words whose regularisations happen to be words in their own right (e.g. GREAT "greet ... hold with somebody ... show them around"). Similarly, why did BS accept 9 out of 15 pseudohomophones as words in the lexical decision task while rejecting all 15 non-homophonic nonwords? An intact orthographic system wired up correctly to semantics should know that BRITE and BRUME are not words, particularly when they are quite different orthographically from BRIGHT and BROOM, yet BS accepted both of those nonwords as words. More generally, if his problem was purely an anomic output problem, why did BS *never* try to show us that he understood *something* of the meaning of irregular words he misread (except when the error was a word in its own right with a meaning of its own, as with GREAT→"greet")? It was not a general characteristic of BS's reaction to items he could not respond to correctly, because he would sometimes go to considerable lengths to show us that he recognised and understood pictures he could not name (e.g. crown→"type of a hat, for a king). That never happened for written words.

It is true that authors such as Van Orden (1987; Van Orden, Johnston, & Hale, 1988) have suggested that direct access to meaning from orthography is considerably less efficient than access to meaning from phonology, and that normal understanding of what a written word means involves considerable use of connections from orthography to phonology and thence to meaning, but we do not accept that BS's problems could be due to any intrinsic inadequacy of the links from orthography to semantics. First, if those links are intrinsically weak, how are normal subjects ever able to comprehend isolated written homophones correctly and ever able to reject pseudohomophones in lexical decision?[3] Second, if direct access to semantics from orthography is so poor, how is it that patients with "word meaning deafness" who fail to comprehend many words they hear, and whose breakdown is widely attributed to a partial disconnection of phonology from semantics, can understand those words when they read them (Franklin, Howard, & Patterson, 1994; Franklin et al., 1995; Franklin, Turner, Lambon Ralph, Morris, & Bailey, 1996)? Finally, why should a brain, which can forge such effective associations between the appearance of faces or objects and the semantic knowledge about those people or things, be so incapable of forging effective associations between written words and their meanings? We are not convinced by any of the arguments which purport to show that direct access to semantics from orthography is less efficient than access to semantics from phonology: hence, we believe that BS's pattern of surface dyslexia cannot be accounted for solely as the result of damage to the links between semantics and phonology.

We propose that damage to the links between orthography and semantics was responsible for BS's visual errors, his problems with homophones and pseudohomophones, and his failure to demonstrate any understanding of the irregular words he misread. We are happy to accept that BS's surface dyslexic tendencies may have been exacerbated by his anomia, but we contend that there was an additional, input aspect to his dyslexia.[4] We would offer the same account of EE (Coltheart & Byng, 1989; Howard & Franklin, 1987), who was also anomic but whose surface dyslexia had input characteristics too. And we would suggest that input damage was the principal cause

---

[3] Van Orden (1987; Van Orden et al., 1988) talks about a "spelling check" being made for homophones, but what is a spelling check if not a set of connections between a word's meaning and its orthography? And if those connections are available for the purpose of checking, why can't they mediate comprehension in the first place?

[4] Therapy which improved his object naming had no effect on his reading, and vice versa. This might be adduced as evidence that his naming and reading problems had different origins. But the two therapies did not even generalise to naming or reading untreated objects or words, so we can conclude nothing from their failure to generalise to the other task. With hindsight, it would have been interesting to train BS on naming objects whose written names he had trouble reading, and to train him on reading the names of objects he had trouble naming, to see if there was item-specific transfer between the two tasks, but we failed to do that.

of the surface dyslexia observed in patients JC (Marshall & Newcombe, 1973; Newcombe & Marshall, 1975, 1981, 1984) and NW (Weekes & Coltheart, 1996) who had, at most, only minimal semantic and word-finding difficulties.[5]

THE TRIANGLE MODEL: GOLDEN OR BERMUDA?

We have almost come to the end of our discussion of surface dyslexia, but before we close we would like to mention two challenges that await the triangle model. The first is those patients we have mentioned earlier who show semantic impairments in the absence of surface dyslexia—patients like WLP (Schwartz et al., 1980), DRN (Cipolotti & Warrington, 1995), and DC (Lambon Ralph et al., 1995). If damage to the semantic system weakens the contribution of the semantic route to reading, thereby revealing the surface dyslexic character of the direct route from orthography to phonology, how is it ever possible to have semantic impairments yet not be surface dyslexic? One possibility considered by Funnell (1996) and Plaut (1997) is that the semantic damage suffered by these patients is not sufficiently severe to reduce the contribution of the semantic route to the point where surface dyslexia emerges. The fact that patient WLP became surface dyslexic as her dementia and her understanding worsened is consistent with this idea. But, as Plaut (1997) notes, there are patients in the literature whose object naming (which, according to the triangle model, involves both semantics and phonology and should therefore be sensitive to damage to both) was no worse than DRN's or DC's, but who were profoundly surface dyslexic (e.g. patient GC of Graham et al., 1994).

Plaut (1997) considers an alternative explanation, which is that individuals may differ in the effectiveness with which the direct route linking orthographic to phonological units operates. He shows that relatively minor changes to some of the parameters that control learning in the triangle model can transform it from one in which the direct route is always dependent upon support from the semantic route for reading low frequency, irregular words into one in which the direct route can learn to read such words unassisted. He proposes that such individual differences may occur in the normal population of readers. Now, we know that normal readers *do* show individual differences in the extent to which they rely upon different routes and procedures, and it would be unreasonable to rule out the possibility that such individual differences could modulate one's response to brain damage. It would be particularly perverse of a discipline like cognitive neuropsychol-

---

[5] Apropos of our discussion of the effect of imageability on BS's surface dyslexia, we note Newcombe and Marshall's (1981, p. 35) observation that "JC does show some tendency to be more accurate with concrete nouns and to be particularly inaccurate with very low-frequency words."

ogy, which places such emphasis upon the subtlest of differences between patients, to deny the potential importance of individual differences in the normal population. The practical problem is that we only see our patients after they have suffered their brain injury, so can only speculate upon differences that may have existed between them when they were fit and well. What we need is for our theories to develop to the point where we can say that if a patient was one type of reader pre-morbidly, then after brain damage they should differ in the following ways from a patient who was previously a different type of reader.

The second challenge to the triangle model is one whose answer might relate to the first one. If anomia is also capable of reducing the semantic contribution to reading aloud, why aren't all anomic patients also surface dyslexic? Again, one might invoke the notion of pre-morbid individual differences—only those normal readers who rely upon the semantic route to bolster their reading of low frequency, irregular words would be prone to become surface dyslexic when they became anomic. Again, we need our theories to develop to the point where they can predict other ways we could differentiate between these people *after* their brain injuries have occurred.

But there is one last possibility we would like to raise. Patterson, Graham, and Hodges (1994) asked their patients with semantic dementia and surface dyslexia to repeat sequences of three or four words. The patients made frequent phonological errors such as repeating "candle, sword, cotton" as "tandle, sword, totton". These errors occurred more often when they were repeating words whose meanings they no longer understood than when they were repeating words whose meaning was still known to them. Patterson et al. suggested that when the phonological system is deprived of semantic input it tends to deteriorate and become prone to error. Whether that is true, or whether knowing the meanings of words you are asked to repeat helps to overcome a tendency to error, the possibility remains that in order to become surface dyslexic you need two things—first, a reduced contribution of semantics to reading caused by a lesion somewhere along the semantic route, and second a phonological impairment which causes the phonological representations of words to come apart.[6] On this view, patients with semantic impairment without surface dyslexia, or anomia without surface dyslexia, would be patients with intact phonological representations who would *not* be prone to the type of repetition errors documented by Patterson et al.

Sadly, DC's dementia has progressed to the point where virtually all she can

---

[6] Funnell (1996) failed to find a difference between her semantic dementia patient EP's ability to repeat words she did or did not understand. There are, however, methodological differences between Funnell's experimental procedure and that of Patterson et al. (1994) that may account for this failure to replicate the Patterson et al. observation (see Funnell, 1996,

do is read aloud: We can no longer communicate to her requirements such as to repeat sequences of words. And we failed to assess BS's repetition of word sequences at the time when we did most of the work with him. But in August 1993, soon after we had first made contact with him, BS could repeat single one-syllable words correctly and also pairs of one-syllable words, but when trying to repeat "bank, club, dark, fun" he said "blank, no", transposing the "l" of "club" into "bank" to make "blank", and when trying to repeat "room, queen, gas, bed" he said "room, guess, bed", composing "guess" out of parts of "gas" and "bed". It may be that BS suffered from the same phonological impairment as Patterson et al.'s (1994) semantic dementia cases, and that the phonological impairment played a role in causing him to be surface dyslexic. That impairment may have arisen at the time when we know that his semantics were not functioning properly, but may not have recovered as his semantics improved. That, alas, is pure speculation.

Marshall and Newcombe (1973) began the study of surface dyslexia. It is clear that we still have some way to go before the job is finished.

ACKNOWLEDGEMENTS

We thank BS and his family for working with us, and hope that we were able to contribute something in return. We also thank Elaine Funnell and John Marshall for comments, and David Plaut and Karalyn Patterson for discussing with us some of the ideas contained in this chapter.

REFERENCES

Behrmann, M., & Bub, D. (1992). Surface dyslexia and dysgraphia: Dual routes, single lexicon. *Cognitive Neuropsychology*, *9*, 209–251.

Behrmann, M., & Byng, S. (1992). A cognitive approach to the neurorehabilitation of acquired language disorders. In D.I. Margolin (Ed.), *Cognitive neuropsychology in clinical practice*. New York: Oxford University Press.

Bird, H., & Franklin, S. (1995–96). Cinderella revisited: A comparison of fluent and non-fluent aphasic speech. *Journal of Neurolinguistics*, *9*, 187–206.

Bub, D., Cancelliere, A., & Kertesz, A. (1985). Whole-word and analytic translation of spelling to sound in a nonsemantic reader. In K. Patterson, J.C. Marshall, & M. Coltheart (Eds), *Surface dyslexia: Neuropsychological and cognitive studies of phonological reading*. Hove, UK: Lawrence Erlbaum Associates Ltd.

Byng, S., & Coltheart, M. (1986). Aphasia therapy research: Methodological requirements and illustrative results. In E. Hjelmquist & L.-G. Nilsson (Eds), *Communication and handicap: Aspects of psychological compensation and technical aids*. Amsterdam: Elsevier Science.

Caramazza, A. (1989). Cognitive neuropsychology and rehabilitation: An unfulfilled promise? In X. Seron & G. Deloche (Eds), *Cognitive approaches in neuropsychological rehabilitation*. Hillsdale, NJ: Lawrence Erlbaum Associates Inc.

Caramazza, A., & Hillis, A.E. (1990). Where do semantic errors come from? *Cortex*, *26*, 95–122.

Cipolotti, L., & Warrington, E.K. (1995). Semantic memory and reading abilities: A case report. *Journal of the International Neuropsychological Society, 1*, 104–110.

Coltheart, M. (1983). Investigating the efficacy of speech therapy. In C. Code & D.J. Muller (Eds.), *Aphasia therapy*. London: Edward Arnold.

Coltheart, M., & Byng, S. (1989). A treatment for surface dyslexia. In X. Seron & G. Deloche (Eds), *Cognitive approaches to neuropsychological rehabilitation* (pp. 159–174). Hillsdale, NJ: Lawrence Erlbaum Associates Inc.

Coltheart, M., Curtis, B., Atkins, P., & Haller, M. (1993). Models of reading aloud: Dual-route and parallel-distributed-processing approaches. *Psychological Review, 100*, 589–608.

Coltheart, M., & Funnell, E. (1987). Reading and writing: One lexicon or two? In D.A. Allport, D.G. Mackay, W. Prinz, & E. Scheerer (Eds), *Language perception and production: Shared mechanisms in listening, speaking, reading and writing*. London: Academic Press.

Coltheart, M., Masterson, J., Byng, S., Prior, M., & Riddoch, J. (1983). Surface dyslexia. *Quarterly Journal of Experimental Psychology, 35A*, 469–495.

Crerar, M.A., Ellis, A.W., & Dean, E.C. (1996). Remediation of sentence processing deficits in aphasia using a computer-based microworld. *Brain and Language, 52*, 229–275.

Ellis, A.W., & Young, A.W. (1988). *Human cognitive neuropsychology*. Hove, UK: Lawrence Erlbaum Associates Ltd.

Franklin, S., Howard, D., & Patterson, K.E. (1994). Abstract word meaning deafness. *Cognitive Neuropsychology, 11*, 1–34.

Franklin, S., Howard, D., & Patterson, K.E. (1995). Abstract word anomia. *Cognitive Neuropsychology, 12*, 549–566.

Franklin, S., Turner, J.M., & Ellis, A.W. (1992). *The ADA comprehension battery*. London: Action for Dysphasic Adults.

Franklin, S., Turner, J.M., Lambon Ralph, M.A., Morris, J., & Bailey, P.J. (1996). A distinctive case of word meaning deafness? *Cognitive Neuropsychology, 13*, 1139–1162.

Funnell, E. (1996). Response biases in oral reading: An account of the co-occurrence of surface dyslexia and semantic dementia. *Quarterly Journal of Experimental Psychology, 49A*, 417–446.

Graham, K.S., Hodges, J.R., & Patterson, K. (1994). The relationship between comprehension and oral reading in progressive fluent aphasia. *Neuropsychologia, 32*, 299–316.

Graham, K.S., Patterson, K., & Hodges, J.R. (1995). Progressive pure anomia: Insufficient activation of phonology by meaning. *Neurocase, 1*, 25–38.

Hillis, A.E. (1993). The role of models of language processing in rehabilitation of language impairments. *Aphasiology, 7*, 5–26.

Hillis, A.E., & Caramazza, A. (1991). Mechanisms for accessing lexical representations for output: Evidence for a category-specific semantic deficit. *Brain and Language, 40*, 106–144.

Howard, D. (1995). Lexical anomia: Or the case of the missing lexical entries. *Quarterly Journal of Experimental Psychology, 48A*, 999–1023.

Howard, D., & Franklin, S. (1987). Three ways for understanding written words, and their use in two contrasting cases of surface dyslexia. In D.A. Allport, D. MacKay, W. Prinz, & E. Scheerer (Eds), *Language perception and production: Relationships between listening, speaking, reading and writing*. London: Academic Press.

Howard, D., & Patterson, K.E. (1992). *The pyramids and palm trees test*. Bury St Edmunds, UK: Thames Valley Test Corporation.

Kay, J. (1992). The write stuff: A case of acquired spelling disorder. In R. Campbell (Ed.), *Mental lives* (pp. 134–149). Oxford, UK: Blackwell.

Kay, J., & Ellis, A.W. (1987). A cognitive neuropsychological case study of anomia. *Brain, 110*, 613–629.

Kay, J., Lesser, R., & Coltheart, M. (1992). *PALPA: Psycholinguistic assessments of language processing in aphasia.* Hove, UK: Lawrence Erlbaum Associates Ltd.

Kay, J., & Patterson, K. (1985). Routes to meaning in surface dyslexia. In K. Patterson, M. Coltheart, & J.C. Marshall (Eds), *Surface dyslexia: Neuropsychological and cognitive studies of phonological reading.* Hove, UK: Lawrence Erlbaum Associates Ltd.

Lambon Ralph, M. A., & Ellis, A. W. (1997). "Patterns of paralexia" revisited: Report of a case of visual dyslexia. *Cognitive Neuropsychology, 14,* 953–974.

Lambon Ralph, M.A., Ellis, A.W., & Franklin, S. (1995). Semantic loss without surface dyslexia. *Neurocase,* 1, 363–369.

Marshall, J.C., & Newcombe, F. (1973). Patterns of paralexia: A psycholinguistic approach. *Journal of Psycholinguistic Research,* 2, 175–199.

McCarthy, R.A., & Warrington, E.K. (1986). Phonological reading: Phenomena and para-doxes. *Cortex,* 22, 359–380.

Morton, J. (1969). Interaction of information in word recognition. *Psychological Review, 76,* 165–178.

Morton, J. (1970). A functional model for memory. In D.A. Norman (Ed.), *Models of human memory.* New York: Academic Press.

Nelson, H.E. (1982). *National adult reading test (NART).* Windsor, UK: NFER-Nelson.

Newcombe, F., & Marshall, J.C (1975). Traumatic dyslexia: Localization and linguistics. In K.J. Zülch, O. Creutzfeldt, & G.C. Galbraith (Eds), *Cerebral localisation.* Berlin, Germany: Springer-Verlag.

Newcombe, F., & Marshall, J.C. (1981). On psycholinguistic classifications of the acquired dyslexias. *Bulletin of the Orton Society, 31,* 29–46.

Newcombe, F., & Marshall, J.C. (1984). Varieties of acquired dyslexia: A linguistic approach. *Seminars in Neurology,* 4, 181–195.

Patterson, K., Graham, N., & Hodges, J.R. (1994). The impact of semantic memory loss on phonological representations. *Journal of Cognitive Neuroscience,* 6, 57–69.

Patterson, K. & Hodges, J.R. (1992). Deterioration of word meaning: Implications for reading. *Neuropsychologia, 30,* 1025–1040.

Patterson, K., Marshall, J.C., & Coltheart, M. (1985). *Surface dyslexia: Neuropsychological and cognitive studies of phonological reading.* London: Lawrence Erlbaum Associates.

Patterson, K., & Morton, J. (1985). From orthography to phonology: An attempt at an old interpretation. In K. Patterson, J.C. Marshall, & M. Coltheart (Eds), *Surface dyslexia: Neuropsychological and cognitive studies of phonological reading.* Hove, UK: Lawrence Erlbaum Associates Ltd.

Patterson, K., Plaut, D.C., McClelland, J.L., Seidenberg, M.S., Behrmann, M., & Hodges, J.R. (1997). Connections and disconnections: A connectionist account of surface dyslexia. In J. Reggia, R. Berndt, & E. Ruppin (Eds), *Neural modeling of cognitive and brain disorders.* New York: World Scientific.

Patterson, K., & Shewell, C. (1987). Speak and spell: Dissociations and word-class effects. In M. Coltheart, R. Job, & G. Sartori (Eds), *The cognitive neuropsychology of language.* Hove, UK: Lawrence Erlbaum Associates Ltd.

Plaut, D.C. (1997). Structure and function in the lexical system: Insights from distributed models of word reading and lexical decision. *Language and Cognitive Processes, 12,* 765–805.

Plaut, D.C., McClelland, J.L., Seidenberg, M.S., & Patterson, K. (1996). Understanding normal and impaired reading: Computational principles in quasi-regular domains. *Psychological Review, 103,* 56–115.

Plaut, D.C., & Shallice, T. (1994). *Connectionist modelling in cognitive neuropsychology: A case study.* Hove, UK: Lawrence Erlbaum Associates Ltd.

Raymer, A.M., & Berndt, R.S. (1994). Models of word reading: Evidence from Alzheimer's disease. *Brain and Language,* 47, 479–482.

Riddoch, M.J., & Humphreys, G.W. (1992). *Birmingham object recognition battery (BORB)*. Hove, UK: Lawrence Erlbaum Associates Ltd.

Saffran, E.M., & Schwartz, M.F. (1994). Of cabbages and things: Semantic memory from a neuropsychological perspective—a tutorial review. In C. Umiltà & M. Moscovitch (Eds), *Attention and performance XV* (pp. 507–536). Cambridge, MA.: MIT Press.

Schwartz, M.F., Saffran, E.M., & Marin, O.S.M. (1980). Fractionating the reading process in dementia: Evidence for word-specific print-to-sound associations. In M. Coltheart, K. Patterson, & J.C. Marshall (Eds), *Deep dyslexia*. London: Routledge & Kegan Paul.

Seidenberg, M.S., Waters, G.S., Barnes, M.A., & Tanenhaus, M.K. (1994). When does irregular spelling or pronunciation influence word recognition? *Journal of Verbal Learning and Verbal Behavior, 23,* 383–404.

Shallice, T. (1988). *From neuropsychology to mental structure*. Cambridge, UK: Cambridge University Press.

Shallice, T., Warrington, E.K., & McCarthy, R. (1983). Reading without semantics. *Quarterly Journal of Experimental Psychology, 35A,* 111–130.

Snodgrass, J.G., & Vanderwart, M. (1980). A standardized set of 260 pictures: Norms for name agreement, image agreement, familiarity, and visual complexity. *Journal of Experimental Psychology: Human Learning and Memory, 6,* 174–215.

Snowling, M., Stothard, S., & McLean, J. (1996). *Graded nonword reading test*. Bury St Edmonds, UK: Thames Valley Test Corporation.

Strain, E., Patterson, K.E., & Seidenberg, M.S. (1994). Semantic effects in single-word naming. *Journal of Experimental Psychology: Learning, Memory and Cognition, 21,* 1140–1154.

Van Orden, G.C. (1987). A rows is a rose: Spelling, sound, and reading. *Memory and Cognition, 15,* 181–198.

Van Orden, G.C., Johnston, J.C., & Hale, B.L. (1988). Word identification in reading proceeds from spelling to sound to meaning. *Journal of Experimental Psychology: Learning, Memory and Cognition, 14,* 371–386.

Weekes, B., & Coltheart, M. (1996). Surface dyslexia and surface dysgraphia: Treatment studies and their theoretical implications. *Cognitive Neuropsychology, 13,* 277–315.

CHAPTER FIVE

Developmental surface dyslexia

Jackie Masterson
University of Essex, Colchester, UK

AN INTRODUCTION TO CD

In 1983, Coltheart, Masterson, Byng, Prior, and Riddoch reported investigations of the reading and spelling performance of CD, a 16-year-old developmental dyslexic. On the basis of their investigations, Coltheart et al. claimed that the form of dyslexia exhibited by CD was surface dyslexia. Publication of the report sparked a debate about the existence of surface dyslexia as a separable sub-type of developmental dyslexia that has continued to the present day. In this chapter we will examine the case reports, group studies, and critiques that have fuelled this discussion.

When Coltheart et al. began testing CD she was 15 years old. However, her reading age was 11;0 and her spelling age was 9;0. She had always experienced great difficulty with reading and spelling at school but the cause of this difficulty was not apparent. CD was of average IQ, and had not experienced any social deprivation or emotional problems. There was no evidence of neurological abnormality and no past history of literacy problems in CD's family, nor had she suffered from a serious illness or language disorder that could have resulted in a problem with reading and spelling. CD therefore appeared to be a classic example of someone who, in every other respect, was developing normally but who was suffering from "unexpected" reading failure.

Coltheart et al. gave CD a range of standardised tests of reading and spelling and found that she was impaired in reading aloud, silent reading comprehension, and written and oral spelling. The contrast between her spoken word comprehension ability and her ability to comprehend from print was demonstrated clearly when she was given both the spoken and written version of the English Picture Vocabulary Test. Her age score equivalent was 17;5 years for the spoken version and 13;2 years for the written version. During early stages of testing it was noted that many of CD's errors in reading and spelling seemed to be "phonically" based (for example, *come* was read aloud as "comb", *shove* as "showve"; "cough" was spelled COF). Coltheart et al. gave CD a number of further tests in order to determine whether her pattern of reading and spelling performance could be described as characteristic of surface dyslexia. The results of this testing will be described after early studies of developmental and acquired surface dyslexia have been discussed, in order to provide the context for the investigations.

EARLY INVESTIGATIONS OF ACQUIRED SURFACE DYSLEXIA

Surface dyslexia was first described in any detail by Marshall and Newcombe (1973) in their seminal paper outlining a classification scheme for the acquired dyslexias. Two of the cases of acquired dyslexia described by Marshall and Newcombe were adults who had suffered brain injury as a result of missile wounds during the Second World War. An analysis of the errors made by the two patients in reading aloud was carried out. Marshall and Newcombe suggested that the procedure used by skilled readers for going directly from visual input addresses to semantic addresses was unavailable to these patients; instead, they were forced to rely on grapheme–phoneme correspondence rules to read, and these were not always applied correctly. Examples of error types reported by Marshall and Newcombe for the patients are: assigning a phonetic value to silent consonants (e.g. *listen*→"liston", *island*→"izland") and stress assignment errors (e.g. *begin*→"beggin").

Shallice and Warrington (1980) were next to provide a report of acquired surface dyslexia (although they used the term "semantic dyslexia" to refer to the disorder). They investigated the reading and spelling of ROG, who had suffered a subarachnoid haemorrhage. Shallice and Warrington demonstrated that ROG had difficulty with printed words with exceptional spelling–sound correspondences by presenting a set of matched exception and regular words for reading aloud. ROG read aloud correctly fewer of the exception words than the regular words. Like the patients of Marshall and Newcombe, ROG's errors included responses which have come to be called "regularisations" (for example, *broad*→/browd/), where it appears as if an exception word has been read aloud using a sub-lexical phonological procedure.

Subsequent investigations and explanations of acquired surface dyslexia (see Chapter 4) were in agreement with Marshall and Newcombe's interpretation in ascribing the disorder to a difficulty in accessing lexical-orthographic representations from print. However, there were diverse views of the procedure used by skilled readers to read when the lexical mechanism is not available (cf. Coltheart, 1981; Marcel, 1980; Shallice, 1981). This meant that the interpretation of the procedure used by surface dyslexics to read aloud also varied. Prevailing views of how a sub-lexical reading procedure might operate were in terms of grapheme–phoneme correspondences,

correspondences between morphemes and phonology, and an analogy mechanism.

SURFACE DYSLEXIA AS A DEVELOPMENTAL DISORDER OF READING

Holmes (1973, 1978) compared the reading performance of the two surface dyslexic patients who were described by Marshall and Newcombe with that of four boys aged between 9 and 13 years who had been diagnosed as developmental dyslexics. Holmes reported that the reading errors of the developmental dyslexics were comparable to those described for the acquired surface dyslexic patients. Responses included failure to apply "rule of e" (e.g. *unite*→"unit", *lace*→"lass"), realisation of silent consonants, use of an incorrect correspondence for a vowel diphthong (e.g. *bread*→"breed"), and incorrect stress assignment.

The approach used by Marshall and Newcombe and by Holmes involved the detailed analysis of error responses and an interpretation of the reading performance based on a model of language processing. Studies of developmental dyslexia being carried out at that time tended to involve comparison of groups of dyslexic and control children on various abilities such as visual memory or auditory-perceptual skills; alternatively, they involved the delineation of sub-groups of dyslexic children on the basis of language test scores, or other performance variables such as intelligence test sub-scale scores, or mathematics ability (e.g. Denckla, 1977, 1978; Kinsbourne & Warrington, 1963; Mattis, French & Rapin, 1975; Smith, 1970). The case study methodology used by Holmes was an alternative to the prevailing group study approach in the field of developmental dyslexia.

Analysis of the reading and spelling errors made by developmental dyslexics had, however, previously been carried out by Boder (1971, 1973), for purposes of sub-group classification. Boder examined the reading and spelling performance of 107 dyslexic children. She delineated a dysphonetic sub-group, which represented 63% of the sample. Children in this sub-group were described as having a limited sight vocabulary but no "word analysis" skills, and were therefore unable to sound out unfamiliar words. This sub-type may be the equivalent of developmental phonological dyslexia (see, for example, Temple & Marshall, 1983; Snowling & Hulme, 1989). A second sub-group delineated by Boder was dyseidetic dyslexia, which accounted for 9% of the sample. The reading performance of children in this sub-group was characterised as a difficulty in learning what words look like so that reading had to proceed by a laborious process of sounding out familiar as well as unfamiliar letter strings. Boder gives examples of the types of reading errors made by dyseidetic dyslexics, for example, *business*→"bussyness", *talk*→"talc". She suggests that dyslexics in this sub-group spell as they read, that is by a process of phonetic analysis, resulting in errors such as "listen"→LISN, "laugh"→LAF, "bird"→BURD. A third, "mixed dysphonetic-dyseidetic" sub-group accounted for the remaining children in Boder's sample. Children in this sub-group were described as having a combination of the deficits of the other two groups and as being more severely impaired in reading and spelling.

The description given by Boder of the reading performance of children in the dyseidetic sub-group is strongly reminiscent of the reading performance described previously for surface dyslexics. However, whereas Boder argues for the use of a particular processing strategy by a child experiencing literacy problems on the basis of a qualitative analysis of errors, more conclusive evidence would come from quantitative data collected on tasks known to tap sub-skills for reading and spelling. This was the approach used by Coltheart et al. (1983) in deciding whether CD's reading and spelling performance could be described as characteristic of surface dyslexia. These investigations are discussed next.

INVESTIGATIONS OF CD'S READING AND SPELLING

Coltheart et al. (1983) claimed that the literature on surface dyslexia indicated that an essential symptom was poor performance in reading irregular or exception words. CD was therefore given 39 regular and 39 irregular words to read aloud. The list of words had been devised by Coltheart, Besner, Jonasson, and Davelaar (1979). Regular and irregular words were matched on a pairwise basis for frequency, number of letters, number of syllables, number of morphemes, imageability, and part of speech. CD read correctly significantly more of the regular words than the irregular words (35/39 and 26/39 respectively). Coltheart et al. compared this level of performance with that of the acquired surface dyslexic patient ROG studied by Shallice and Warrington (1980). ROG read aloud 36/39 regular words and 25/39 irregular words.

The regularity effect shown by CD was examined further in a reading task that required the conversion of print to phonology but did not require spoken responses. CD was asked to decide whether pairs of letter strings had identical or different pronunciations in a silent homophony judgement task. Three different forms of the task were used: a regular word version, an irregular word version, and a nonword version. In each test half of the 50 letter-string pairs sounded identical (e.g. *hair/hare*, *fid/phid*) and half did not (e.g. *hair/hard*, *fid/prid*). The orthographic overlap (or spelling similarity) of the "same" and "different" pairs was matched so that the task could not be completed on the basis of the greater visual similarity of the homophonic pairs. CD correctly judged 44/50 regular pairs, 39/50 nonword pairs, and 34/50 irregular pairs. The level of performance on the three different tests was significantly different and performance was significantly worse on the irregular version than on the regular version.

Coltheart et al. had therefore demonstrated that CD showed worse performance with irregular words than regular words in both reading aloud and silent reading. They analysed the errors CD made in reading aloud. Examples of both regularisation and stress assignment errors were found in CD's responses, as had been reported for the acquired surface dyslexics studied by Marshall and Newcombe (1973). Coltheart et al. argued that CD's regularisation errors, such as *bear*→"beer", *gauge*→"gorge", were the result of the application of grapheme–phoneme correspondence rules, which were used when access to word-specific representations was not possible. Likewise, stress assignment errors were made because of the irregular nature of stress assignment for polysyllabic words in English—the only way to ensure correct stress assignment would be to use word-specific information. Finally, Coltheart et al. observed visual errors in CD's reading aloud responses (e.g. *frog*→"fog", *topic*→"tropic"), and these had also been reported for the acquired surface dyslexics studied by Marshall and Newcombe (1973) and the developmental dyslexics studied by Holmes (1973).

Given that CD's reading responses to irregular words were often regularisation errors, it was of interest to discover how these words were comprehended. Coltheart et al. investigated CD's reading comprehension by asking her to define words as well as read them aloud. They found that CD's definitions corresponded to her oral reading responses on the vast majority of occasions, irrespective of whether the word was read aloud correctly or not. Thus, of 95 trials CD read and defined 49 words correctly and read 46 words incorrectly. Of the 46 incorrect responses, 44 were defined according to the subsequent reading response (e.g. *bear*→"a drink ... beer", *enigma*→"a picture ... image"). There were only four occasions in the 95 trials when CD's definition and subsequent reading response did not match (e.g. *debt*→"when you owe something ... depth", *surplus*→"some news, a surplus which goes around ... surplus").

Coltheart et al. studied CD's spelling errors in written and oral spelling tasks and observed that 60% were phonologically correct. All of the features of reading and spelling performance reported for CD were also observed by Coltheart et al. for an acquired dyslexic patient, AB.

Coltheart et al. interpreted CD's reading problem in the context of the logogen model put forward by Morton and Patterson (1980). They concluded that the results from the reading tasks show that CD had a deficit at the level of the visual input logogen system: when a representation was unavailable in this system CD was forced to rely on the phonological representation of the word for reading, and this was derived using grapheme–phoneme correspondence rules. This resulted in worse performance for irregular words. When the task was reading comprehension and a representation was unavailable in the input logogen system, the cognitive system had to be accessed using a phonological representation—the equivalent of understanding a heard word. This type of mediation would only be successful if the printed word was regular and not a homophone. Comprehension of an irregular word would be incorrect because the phonological representation produced by grapheme–phoneme rules would be incorrect. Homophones would be a source of difficulty in the comprehension task when their representations were unavailable in the visual input logogen system because the phonological representation derived using grapheme–phoneme correspondences is ambiguous for homophones. If this representation were to be used to access the cognitive system then a homophone confusion error would be likely to occur. A number of the words that had been presented to CD in the comprehension task were homophones. Coltheart et al. observed that CD made many homophone confusion errors (e.g. *pane*→"something which hurts").

The investigations of CD's reading and spelling behaviour thus provided both qualitative as well as quantitative means for diagnosing developmental surface dyslexia. However, a number of authors did not agree that surface dyslexia had been convincingly demonstrated to exist as a developmental disorder. Their objections are outlined next.

OBJECTIONS TO COMPARISONS OF ACQUIRED AND DEVELOPMENTAL SURFACE DYSLEXIA

In the same year that Coltheart et al. published their investigations of CD's reading and spelling, Temple and Marshall (1983) reported the case of HM, a 17-year-old girl whose reading was characterised by a deficit in sub-lexical phonological skill. Temple and Marshall concluded that HM represented a case of developmental phonological dyslexia, by analogy with previously reported cases of acquired phonological dyslexia. Bryant and Impey (1986) argued that, in drawing comparisons between the reading of individuals with developmental and acquired dyslexia, Coltheart et al. (1983) and Temple and Marshall (1983) had failed to take into account the variation in reading strategies shown by children learning to read normally. They gave the tasks used by Coltheart et al. and by Temple and Marshall to a group of 16 6- to 11-year-old children who had a mean reading age of 10 years. This reading age was chosen because it was equivalent to the reading age of both of the developmental dyslexics studied by Coltheart et al. and Temple and Marshall.

Bryant and Impey found that features of surface dyslexia, such as lower accuracy in reading irregular compared to regular words, regularisation errors, and homophone confusions, were also characteristic of the reading of the group of normal readers. The only apparent difference in the performance of the normal readers and the two developmental dyslexics HM and CD was in nonword reading—the normal readers appeared to be able to read nonwords with greater accuracy than either HM or CD. Correlational analyses revealed that there was a negative correlation between incidence of "surface symptoms" and "phonological symptoms" in the results of the normal readers. Bryant and Impey decided to see if there were extreme cases in the normal group who were like CD and HM. They report two cases who showed a pattern similar to HM and one case who resembled the pattern of reading shown by CD. The latter child made many regularisation errors and had difficulty reading irregular words; however, nonword reading accuracy was good, in contrast to CD's poor performance in reading nonwords.

As we saw previously, Coltheart et al. had interpreted CD's reading problem in terms of a partial defect in the input logogen system. Bryant and Impey argue that this interpretation of developmental surface dyslexia as a defect of development of the "functional architecture" needed for skilled reading was mistaken. This was because they had shown that the features of surface dyslexia exist in children who were learning to read normally. They suggest therefore that CD's pattern of reading provides no evidence for any specific defect since it is shown by children who do not have reading disorder.

Temple (1987) argued that Bryant and Impey had not provided a good reading age match for CD or HM in their group of normal readers. Temple also pointed out that no account had been taken of the range of chronological age (6;3–11;9 years) of the children in Bryant and Impey's sample. Given that the average reading age in the group was 10 years, this means that there were young children in the group with a very advanced level of reading ability and older children with low levels of reading ability who may have been dyslexic. Temple therefore considered that Bryant and Impey's criticisms of the studies comparing acquired and developmental forms of dyslexia were undermined by the lack of appropriate reading level controls for the two developmental dyslexics.

There have been a number of studies of reading development in young children, apart from that of Bryant and Impey, that have used similar tasks and materials to those used by Coltheart et al. and Temple and Marshall. These have allowed a clearer picture to emerge of the similarities between surface dyslexia and normal beginning reading. For example, Backman, Bruck, Hebert, and Seidenberg (1984) and Waters, Seidenberg, and Bruck (1984) reported regularity effects in the reading of children in Grades 2–4; Masterson (1983) and Masterson, Laxon, and Stuart (1992) investigated the reading of 5- and 6-year-old children and found evidence of regularity effects, regularisation errors, stress assignment errors, and visual errors; in addition, they found that, as with CD, reading comprehension corresponded with oral reading responses and that homophone confusion errors were common.

Coltheart (1987) pointed out that the findings of Bryant and Impey and of these other studies of young children's reading were actually predicted by Coltheart et al. (1983, p. 486): "There will be many quite common irregular words which will be unfamiliar to the young normal reader, and since young normal readers will have a good knowledge of the orthographic-phonological correspondences of English ... regularisation errors will be frequent when young normal readers are reading irregular words aloud ... It would not be at all surprising ... if most or all of the symptoms of surface dyslexia could be found in young normal readers ..." (p. 486). Coltheart (1987) disputes Bryant and Impey's suggestion that, because CD's reading pattern is found in normal readers of equivalent reading age, then it is not abnormal. He argues that it would only be normal if she was in fact much younger. That is, CD's reading was abnormal because most children develop lexical–orthographic representations over the course of repeated exposure to printed words; by the time they are 16, as CD was, they have left behind the stage of pronounced use of sub-lexical phonology. CD's reading performance, marked by such features as regularisations and homophone confusions, showed that she was still at this stage. Her reading was therefore abnormal because she had been unable to fully develop a lexical procedure, despite many years of exposure to printed words.

Further criticisms of the conclusions drawn by Coltheart et al. (1983) came from Wilding (1989). He argued that the classification of CD as a developmental surface dyslexic was unsatisfactory on a number of grounds. The first objection raised was that specific cut-off points for delineating performance on the tasks given to CD were not provided by Coltheart et al. Wilding suggests that the relative frequencies of different error types made by CD cannot justify her classification as a surface dyslexic without a proper sample of the relevant population. Wilding also argues that the error data provided by Holmes (1973) show evidence of both lexical and sub-lexical involvement in the reading of the children, which is inconsistent with their classification as developmental surface dyslexics. He suggests that some of the reading responses appear to be the result of faulty matching to sight vocabulary (for example, *beauty*→"dirty", *gnome*→"gum", *argue*→"angry") rather than the use of a sub-lexical phonological reading strategy. Wilding points out that many of the errors reported by Coltheart et al. for CD also show evidence of the operation of processes other than sub-lexical phonology. Finally, he suggests that since CD had poor nonword reading skills then her reading difficulty is basically the same as that of developmental phonological dyslexics; that is, she has a basic weakness in phonological processing.

In a sequel paper, Wilding (1990) suggests that apparent differences between developmental dyslexics are due to differences in strategy use resulting from instruction, or else are due to different methods that the dyslexics have adopted for coping with the problem (see Snowling, 1983, for a similar argument). We will now examine further reports of developmental surface dyslexia to see whether more recent studies have satisfactorily dealt with the criticisms outlined earlier.

FURTHER CASES OF DEVELOPMENTAL SURFACE DYSLEXIA

Three further cases of developmental surface dyslexia were reported by Masterson (1984). CD was also reported in this paper. The reading performance of the four developmental dyslexics was compared to that of five acquired surface dyslexic patients. Two of the developmental dyslexics were younger than CD, both 10 years old, and the fourth was 26 years old. Reading ages of the two younger dyslexics were 7 years and 8 years, and that of the older dyslexic 12 years. The only individual to have received remedial help was KW, one of the younger dyslexics. The remediation received by KW had been phonics-based and of 2 years' duration prior to testing. The acquired surface dyslexics were aged 16–54 years. Four had sustained traumatic brain injury and the fifth had suffered a stroke. The nine dyslexics were given the Coltheart et al. (1979) list of regular and irregular words for reading aloud and all showed a significant regularity effect. In the case of the developmental dyslexics, this was most marked for KW who read 77% of regular words and only 28% of irregular words correctly. It was argued that this extreme regularity effect may have been due to the phonics-based remediation that KW had received. However, effects of remediation could not be invoked as an explanation for the regularity effects shown by the other developmental dyslexics.

An analysis of the errors made on the Coltheart et al. list revealed that there was a strong level of agreement in the irregular words found difficult by the acquired and developmental dyslexics. All of them made regularisation errors and visual errors. The four developmental dyslexics were also found to show very similar levels of performance to those of the acquired dyslexics on the silent homophony judgement tests described earlier in the section outlining tests given to CD. The spelling errors of the nine dyslexics were mostly phonologically appropriate, and homophone confusions were also reported for all nine in a printed word definition task. Thus, all of the characteristics previously reported for acquired surface dyslexia were observed for the developmental dyslexics in the study.

Temple (1984) described three cases of developmental dyslexia, AH, MH, and RB, who were well matched in terms of chronological age and literacy skills. All were aged 10 years, all had reading comprehension ages of 10 years, reading accuracy ages of 8 years, and spelling ages of 7 years. All were of above average intelligence and had extensive receptive vocabularies. Two of the children showed significantly poorer performance when reading nonwords compared to words. The third, RB, did not show an accuracy difference in reading words and nonwords but showed a significant regularity effect when reading aloud the Coltheart et al. (1979) list. AH and MH did not read significantly more of the regular than the irregular words aloud. Temple suggested that RB was surface dyslexic and the other two dyslexics were developmental phonological dyslexics.

Temple carried out further investigations of the reading of the three developmental dyslexics. It was argued that the proportion of neologistic to paralexic reading errors should be higher for surface dyslexics than for phonological dyslexics since the former often rely on a phonological recoding strategy, whereas the latter do not. The proportion of neologistic errors was 64% for RB and 42% and 31% for the other two dyslexics. In addition, Temple reports that RB was unaffected by stimulus distortion (words presented with the letters in reverse order), whereas for AH and MH reading performance was significantly reduced. Stimulus distortion had previously been shown to affect the reading performance of an acquired phonological dyslexic by Beauvois and Derousné (1979), presumably due to the disruptive effect it had on a global strategy for reading. Temple also tested the three developmental dyslexics with a homophone definition task. RB defined half of the homophones she read aloud correctly as their respective homophones. However, there were few instances of homophone confusion for AH and MH.

A further four cases of developmental surface dyslexia are described in Temple (1985). Their reading problems are interpreted in terms of problems with parsing, translation, and blending within the sub-lexical procedure. The first case, NG, was 13 years old. His error responses were interpreted by Temple as being valid translation errors (e.g. *borough*→"borrow"; *ough* as in "dough") and blending errors with long words (e.g. *individual*→"invidual"). PhB and SL were both 12 years old. PhB produced errors that resembled the pattern seen for NG, but SL produced errors that Temple suggested represent a difficulty in parsing (e.g. *fancy*→"fankay"). The final case, PB, was a 10-year-old dyslexic who produced errors of parsing (e.g. *either*→"eat her"), translation (e.g. *clear*→"slurch"), and blending (e.g. *digest*→"jest").

Seymour (1986, 1987a) used methods similar to those used by Coltheart et al. (1983) and Temple (1984, 1985) to examine the reading of a series of developmental dyslexics. Reaction time and accuracy data were collected, in addition to control data, for all tasks. The aim was to establish a definition of efficient performance on the tasks, in order to be able to delineate inefficient processing in the developmental dyslexics. Seymour elaborated a theoretical framework for the studies which shared many of the processing systems of the "dual-route" framework that had been used by Coltheart et al. and by Temple, but which emphasised the operation of an "orthographic processor". This is described as a visual system, specialised for the analysis of print, and consisting of two levels. The first of these is an orthographic parser, and the second is responsible for the categorisation and identification of graphemes and morphemes.

Seymour reported developmental dyslexics whose reading of irregular words was impaired in comparison to control performance. He also observed word frequency effects, dispersion of reaction time distribution, and length effects in the reaction time data of these dyslexics. Seymour suggested that the impaired function was the orthographic processor. He used the term "morphemic dyslexia" to refer to these cases.

Seymour and Evans (1993) looked in more detail at the possibility of an orthographic processing deficit in morphemic dyslexia. Two tasks were used to assess the functioning of the orthographic processor. One was an identity judgement task where a row of letters of varying length was displayed. The task involved indicating whether or not all the letters were the same according to a physical identity or nominal identity criterion. Previous studies had indicated that reaction time in this task is independent of array size in skilled readers. This was taken to reflect an early parallel processing stage of the orthographic processor by Seymour and Evans. In the second task two arrays were presented simultaneously and the instructions were to indicate whether or not they were the same. The position of a single difference varied in the array. Seymour and Evans suggested that this requires an analytic point-by-point comparison as indicated by the effects on reaction time in skilled readers of variations in array size and number or position of differences.

Eight dyslexics showing a morphemic pattern (word frequency effect, slow, dispersed reaction time distribution, and length effect) were identified. They demonstrated large regularity effects and made regularisation errors. Seymour and Evans suggest that an orthographic processor impairment might well be expected in morphemic dyslexia since the disorder is characterised by a difficulty in recognising whole words and a commitment to a slow serial form of processing. Results for four of the dyslexics were consistent with this view since they made more errors, or had longer reaction times, than controls in the identity-matching task. However, the suggestion did not receive general support because the performance of four of the dyslexics fell within the range for the controls on the task.

The results suggested, then, that an impairment of the orthographic processor is not necessarily associated with morphemic dyslexia. However, Seymour & Evans suggest that alternative measures of visual orthographic functioning may produce different results. They draw attention to the results of three of the dyslexics studied by Seymour (1986) who had reasonably efficient reading processes but showed a lack of word specific knowledge in spelling and a tendency to produce phonologically appropriate spellings (i.e., a surface dysgraphic pattern). The three children showed reaction time delays in same–different matching and in reading distorted words, particularly when vertical format was used. Seymour & Evans suggest, therefore, that an impairment of the orthographic processor may have severe consequences for spelling rather than for reading.

The detailed work of Seymour and his colleagues provides further evidence that some developmental dyslexics can have a selective deficit of lexical–orthographic functioning, as Coltheart et al. (1983) had attempted to show in their investigations with CD.

DEVELOPMENTAL SURFACE DYSLEXIA IN LANGUAGES OTHER THAN ENGLISH

There have been two reports of cases of developmental surface dyslexia in languages other than English. The first of these was reported by Job, Sartori, Masterson, and Coltheart (1984). Job et al. pointed out that surface dyslexia should not be observed in readers of languages such as Italian which have a regular one-to-one grapheme–phoneme correspondence system, since the hallmark symptoms of surface dyslexia are a difficulty reading irregular words and a comprehension problem with printed homophones. In languages with regular orthographies it should be possible to read all words correctly using a sub-lexical phonological procedure. However, Job et al. argue that a further symptom of surface dyslexia, stress assignment errors, can occur in regular orthographies provided that the language has an irregular stress assignment system. Italian is one of these languages. It has a "free stress" system (Lepschy & Lepschy, 1981) with some polysyllabic words stressed on the first syllable, some on the last syllable, and some on one of the intermediate syllables. However, most Italian words are stressed on the penultimate syllable. Job et al. suggested that since word-specific information such as stress assignment is sometimes not available for surface dyslexics, then the disorder should be manifest in Italian readers by the presence of stress errors, particularly to words that do not have stress on the penultimate syllable.

Job et al. gave Luigi, an 11-year-old Italian developmental dyslexic, lists of words and nonwords to read aloud. They found that he made visual errors consisting of the substitution, insertion, or deletion of one or more letters, or a combination of these. He also made errors that consisted of assigning the stress in irregularly stressed words to the penultimate syllable. A further test was constructed based on the fact that in Italian certain printed sequences of articles and nouns sound the same as other words in the language (for example, *l'ago* (the needle) and *lago* (lake) are pronounced in the same way). A list of 16 such pairs was devised. When Luigi was tested for his comprehension of the stimuli his performance was at chance. Job et al. concluded that Luigi was relying on phonological, and not lexical–orthographic representations, to retrieve the meaning of some words.

A spelling to dictation task was next presented to Luigi using materials from the preceding task. His performance was once again at chance. On half the trials he wrote the homophonic equivalent of the target. Thus, in both reading and spelling tasks Job et al. demonstrated that Luigi was unable to access lexical–orthographic representations for many words, and the pattern of performance was equivalent to that demonstrated by English developmental surface dyslexics.

The second case of developmental surface dyslexia in a language other than English was reported by Masterson, Coltheart, and Meara (1985). Masterson et al. report the case of FE, a 20-year-old Spanish–English bilingual dyslexic. Like Italian, Spanish has a regular one-to-one system of grapheme–phoneme correspondences and so it does not have any irregular words. However, Spanish is not regular with respect to sound–spelling rules, at least as far as Latin American Spanish is concerned, because there are some phonemes that can be spelled in more than one way (for example, *b* and *v* are pronounced identically). This means that there are homophones in written Spanish and so there is the potential for homophone confusion errors to be made. There is also the potential for phonological spelling errors to occur.

FE was tested in English using the list of regular and irregular words from Coltheart et al. (1979). He showed a significant regularity effect and made regularisation errors in reading aloud. More than half of FE's spelling errors in a spelling to dictation task were phonologically appropriate. A homophone comprehension task was devised where a spoken definition was presented together with four printed words. The four words consisted of the word that correctly matched the spoken definition, a homophone of the target, and two further words that were visually similar to the target and its homophone. FE was asked to select the printed word that matched the spoken definition. There were 100 trials and FE made 41 errors. Ten were failures to respond and twenty were choices of the homophone of the correct word. The remaining 11 errors were choice of a visual distractor. Thus, when reading and writing in English, FE showed the hallmark symptoms of developmental surface dyslexia: a regularity effect in reading aloud, phonologically appropriate errors in spelling to dictation, and a tendency to make homophone confusion errors in a printed word comprehension task.

FE was a speaker of Latin American Spanish and it was therefore possible to present him with a homophone definition task in Spanish. Twenty pairs of homophones were selected and the items were presented for definition in two testing sessions. The two members of the homophone pairs were presented in separate sessions. Of the 40 items, 16 were correctly defined, 10 elicited the response "don't know", 2 were inappropriately defined, and 12 resulted in homophone confusions. In spelling Spanish words to dictation, FE made a large number (9/14) of phonologically appropriate spelling errors. Masterson et al. concluded that FE was surface dyslexic in both Spanish and English. They suggest that if further cases of developmental surface dyslexia are found where the symptoms are apparent in both languages then this will indicate that the lexical–orthographic system is not language-specific in polyglot readers, but is used for reading all languages in which the polyglot is competent.

STUDIES OF ADULT DEVELOPMENTAL SURFACE DYSLEXICS

A case report of an adult with developmental surface dyslexia was provided by Goulandris and Snowling (1991). They investigated the reading and spelling of an undergraduate student, JAS. JAS showed a significant regularity effect in reading aloud a list of low frequency words drawn from Boder and Jarrico's (1982) reading test. Goulandris and Snowling also observed a marked preponderance of phonologically appropriate spelling errors in JAS's written work. Nonword reading performance was good and within previously reported limits of the normal range for adults. Performance on a task requiring the selection of an appropriate homophone to match a definition given by the tester was very poor (68% correct). Goulandris and Snowling contrast this result with that obtained for JM, a developmental phonological dyslexic studied by Snowling and Hulme (1989). JM had a reading age of 10 years, whereas JAS had a reading age of 12;6. However, JM was able to select homophones to match spoken definitions with 90% accuracy, highlighting the very different processing impairments in the two dyslexics.

JAS made visual errors in reading words with close orthographic neighbours (e.g. *think*→"thick", *stain*→"strain"). Errors of this kind were taken to indicate that JAS was accessing lexical entries using only partial information, and that a search for an entry in the orthographic lexicon was made before any resort to sub-lexical phonology. Goulandris and Snowling gave JAS a lexical decision task in which half the nonwords were pseudohomophones. She made a high number of false positive responses with the pseudohomophones. The authors suggested that the high false alarm rate was the result of JAS having poorly specified lexical entries, which meant that she needed to resort to using sub-lexical phonology in the lexical decision task to provide information about the lexical status of the letter strings.

Goulandris and Snowling investigated the possibility that a visual perceptual or visual memory impairment might be the cause of the poor function-ing of the lexical procedure observed in JAS. They found that her performance was very poor on standardised tests of visual recognition and recall of designs. A further test was given of memory for letter-like forms. The stimuli were Greek letters which were presented in sequences of two, three, or four letters for 10 sec. JAS was required to select the letters from an array and to place them in the correct (presentation) order. She was unable to obtain a score on any trials in this task. Her performance was compared to that of a group of children with a spelling age of 7 years who obtained an average of 4/12 correct. Goulandris and Snowling suggest that an inability to memorise graphemic information, such as that found for JAS, would prevent the establishment of detailed lexical representations for printed words in the course of learning to read.

A further case study of developmental surface dyslexia in an adult was reported by Hanley, Hastie, and Kay (1992). Allan was 22 years old and is reported as having nonword reading ability comparable to that reported for groups of adults in other studies. He made homophone confusion errors in a printed word definition task, and also made regularisation and visual errors in reading aloud, although reading errors were rare. However, Allan's spelling was much more severely impaired than his reading. Hanley et al. report that there was a marked tendency for spelling errors to be phonologically appropri-ate. Ninety-two per cent of Allan's spelling errors on a list of regular and irregular words taken from the PALPA test battery (Kay, Lesser, & Coltheart, 1992) were phonologically appropriate. Hanley et al. compared the errors to those made by spelling-age-matched control children aged 8 to 9 years. The errors of the controls appeared to involve, in the main, attempts to remember an unusual spelling (e.g. "soldier"→SOLDER, SOLIDER), whereas Allan's errors typically involved preservation of the phonology of the printed word (e.g. "soldier"→SOLDURE). Allan showed a very similar pattern of perfor-mance to JAS (Goulandris & Snowling, 1991, reported previously) on tests of reading and spelling. However, unlike JAS, Allan showed no evidence of a visual memory difficulty on visual retention and recognition tests. Therefore a visual memory impairment may not be a general cause of developmental surface dyslexia.

Hanley et al. gave Allan a task used by Friedrich, Walker, and Posner (1985) to investigate word recognition in patients with parietal lobe damage. As in Seymour and Evans' array matching task described earlier, the task involved deciding whether two simultaneously presented letter strings were the same or different. Control participants were observed by Friedrich et al. to respond more quickly on different trials when the mismatch occurred at the start or end of the letter strings, rather than in the middle. This was interpreted as consistent with an "ends-in" processing strategy. The control participants were also faster to respond when the letter strings were words rather than nonwords (a "word superiority" effect). Allan showed the word superiority effect previously found for controls. He also responded relatively speedily, although he was more error-prone than the controls tested by Friedrich et al. However, he showed no evidence of processing the strings in an "ends-in" fashion. Instead, he appeared to be using a serial left-to-right processing strategy since his decision times on different trials increased in a linear fashion across the mismatch positions. Hanley et al. suggested that the results from this task provided further evidence that Allan was not reading words in the same way as skilled readers.

Hanley et al. suggested that Allan's disorder is consistent with Frith's (1985) stage model of reading acquisition. A child at Frith's second, alphabetic, stage of development would be able to read many irregular words using skills developed previously in the logographic stage. Spelling rather than reading would be seriously hampered by a failure to progress from the alphabetic phase to a final orthographic stage, where fully specified lexical entries are used for reading and spelling. This is because there are many more ways of writing English phonemes than there are of pronouncing them. Thus, some words that are regular for the purposes of reading are irregular for spelling. A reliance on alphabetic skills would therefore have a more obvious consequence for spelling than for reading. Goulandris and Snowling (1991) had previously suggested that the comparable symptoms of JAS were compatible with both Frith's developmental model and with a dual-route model of reading. In terms of the latter framework, they suggested that JAS's pronounced spelling difficulty was likely to be a consequence of poorly specified representations in the orthographic lexicon. Although these representations would often be sufficient for reading, more precise detail is needed for correct spelling and so in an individual with this kind of processing difficulty poor spelling would be particularly apparent. Thus, both stage models of reading development and dual-route models of adult reading appear to be able to provide an account of developmental surface dyslexia and dysgraphia in these adult dyslexics.

A final case study of an adult with developmental surface dyslexia appears in Hanley and Gard (1995). These authors compared the reading and spelling of two adult dyslexic undergraduate students, Mandy and Gregory, who were closely matched on overall level of reading and spelling ability. They were tested on a range of tasks that were also administered to undergraduate control participants. On a test of nonword reading Gregory showed a level of accuracy that was below the range of the controls, whereas Mandy was unimpaired on the task. In reading regularly and irregularly spelled homophones Mandy showed a significant regularity effect. Virtually all of her errors were confined to lower frequency homophones. Gregory made only two errors in reading the list of homophones. In spelling, 84% of the errors made by Mandy were phonologically appropriate, whereas only 60% of Gregory's errors were phonologically appropriate. A list of regular and irregular words was administered for spelling to dictation. On this test it was found that both Mandy and Gregory were significantly affected by spelling regularity. This result was unexpected since Gregory had shown all of the features of developmental phonological dyslexia on the other reading and spelling tasks. If, as suggested by his performance on these other tasks, his sub-lexical skills were inadequate then a regularity effect for spelling should not have been found. Hanley and Gard suggest that the unexpected result might be due to the fact that irregular words are more difficult to learn (presumably by means of a whole-word strategy) than regular words, and so a person who is forced to rely on a lexical strategy during reading and spelling development might show worse performance as an adult when spelling irregular words. A nonword spelling to dictation test was also administered; Gregory scored outside the range for the controls but, once again, Mandy showed unimpaired nonword performance.

Hanley (1997) has reported a study of 33 dyslexic undergraduate students where he assessed their reading and spelling of regular and irregular words and nonwords, lexical decision, and homophone definition. Reading-related "phonological awareness" skills (such as rhyme detection and phoneme counting) were also measured. The performance of the dyslexics on the tasks was compared to that of undergraduates with no reading problems. Hanley reports that 30/33 of the dyslexics were impaired on nonword reading/spelling or on the phonological awareness tasks. Only three of the dyslexics in the sample showed the profile of surface dyslexia, suggesting that this form of developmental dyslexia may be rare. However, the preponderance of one type of pattern of performance is likely to depend on a number of factors, including the criteria used for classifying individuals as dyslexic (Hanley used 2 standard deviations below the mean on standardised tests of reading and spelling), characteristics of the sample (all of the participants in the Hanley study were undergraduate students and therefore likely to be of high general ability level), as well as the types of stimuli and selection of tasks used to assess lexical and sub-lexical reading skills. Given these facts, it seems premature to draw conclusions about the relative frequencies of different types of dyslexia amongst adult dyslexics until further research is carried out.

In conclusion, these recent studies of adults who show the characteristic reading and spelling pattern of developmental surface dyslexia have demonstrated that the disorder can occur in a relatively "pure" form. That is, the reports demonstrate that JAS, Allan, and Mandy have sub-lexical skills that are as efficient as those of adult, skilled readers and that they have a reading and spelling deficit that is restricted to lexical processing only.

THE SUB-GROUPING STUDY OF CASTLES AND
COLTHEART (1993)

Castles and Coltheart (1993) carried out a study that aimed to provide clear evidence for a distinction in symptom pattern between developmental surface and phonological dyslexia. They tested 56 dyslexic boys who ranged in age from 8;6 to 14;11 and who all had reading ages at least 18 months behind their chronological ages. All were within the normal IQ range. Fifty-six control children were selected. They were all boys and ranged in age from 7;6 to 14;0. Their reading ages fell within 6 months of their chronological ages.

The children in both groups were given regular words, irregular words, and nonwords to read aloud. Before the results for the dyslexics were analysed, Castles and Coltheart performed regression analyses of irregular word reading as a function of chronological age, and nonword reading as a function of chronological age, in order to obtain a picture of the normal development of the reading of irregular words and nonwords. There was a highly significant linear relationship between chronological age and irregular word reading and between chronological age and nonword reading. These analyses were used as the basis for the selection of those children in the dyslexic sample who were particularly poor for their age at irregular word reading and/or nonword reading. Upper and lower confidence limits were established for both irregular word and nonword reading, and these were used as the criteria for the selection of extreme scores in the dyslexic group. Scores for 40 dyslexic children fell below the lower confidence limit for irregular word reading, and for nonword reading, scores for 38 dyslexics fell below the lower confidence limit. More importantly, 18 of the dyslexics fell below the lower confidence limit for one of the tasks but were within the limits for the other. Ten were outside the range for irregular word reading, but within the range for nonword reading. In six of these ten cases, nonword reading scores were within 1 standard deviation of the expected score for their age. Eight children showed the reverse pattern, with scores within the expected range for irregular word reading and outside it for nonword reading.

In addition to identifying dyslexics who showed normal performance on one of the tasks and abnormal performance on the other, Castles and Coltheart isolated children who were poor on both tasks, but markedly worse on one compared to the other. It was suggested that these children could also be classified as showing a dissociation between irregular word reading and nonword reading. To achieve this aim a regression of irregular word reading score on nonword reading score was performed for the control children's data. This was carried out in order to estimate the expected number of nonwords that could be read correctly at varying levels of irregular word reading, and vice versa. A significant linear relationship was found, and predicted values were used to identify children in the dyslexic group who were performing below expectation on one task on the basis of their performance on the other task. Results of the analysis revealed that 16 dyslexic children were below the lower confidence limit for irregular word reading when predictions were made from their nonword reading performance. Conversely, 29 fell below the confidence limit for nonword reading when predictions were made from their irregular word reading scores.

Thus, Castles and Coltheart demonstrated that of the 45 children in their dyslexic sample who showed a dissociation between irregular and nonword reading, 29 showed the pattern characteristic of phonological dyslexia and 16 showed the pattern characteristic of surface dyslexia. In a second experiment, Castles and Coltheart examined the auditory comprehension of regular and irregular words by dyslexics showing the surface dyslexic pattern. This was carried out in order to examine the possibility that developmental surface dyslexia involves a general problem in understanding irregular words in spoken language. However, no auditory comprehension difficulties with irregular words could be found and so the authors concluded that developmental surface dyslexia is not due to a general language deficit.

We saw earlier that Wilding (1989) argued that cases of clear dissociation on the critical error categories of irregular word reading and nonword reading had not been demonstrated. Wilding concluded that diagnoses have been made on the basis of relative superiority on one task over the other without any consideration of absolute levels of performance. Castles and Coltheart argue that their results challenge this criticism, since they found many examples of children who fell within the normal range for their age on one skill while they were extremely poor on the other. However, Manis, Seidenberg, Doi, McBride-Chang, and Petersen (1996) and Stanovich, Siegel, and Gottardo (1997) have objected to the treatment of the results in the Castles and Coltheart study. Both sets of authors carried out studies of nonword and irregular word reading in developmental dyslexics using reading age controls as well as chronological age controls (Castles and Coltheart had only used the latter). They also reanalysed the results of Castles and Coltheart but used a reading age matched comparison group. Using the same regression techniques that had been used by Castles and Coltheart, they found that most of the cases of developmental surface dyslexia that were apparent when chronological age control data was used fell within the range of normal performance when reading age control data was used.

We saw earlier that Coltheart (1987) argued that Coltheart et al. (1983) had predicted that the pattern of reading in developmental surface dyslexia would resemble that of younger normal readers and so the results obtained by Manis et al. and Stanovich et al. in the reanalyses of the Castles and Coltheart data using reading-age-matched control data are perhaps not surprising. In the empirical studies carried out by Manis et al. and Stanovich et al., lower rates of incidence of children with extreme discrepancies between nonword reading and irregular word reading were observed (i.e. indicative of phonological or surface dyslexia) compared to the rates of incidence reported by Castles and Coltheart. However, the studies differ in a number of ways, which may indicate that the findings are not comparable. The 56 dyslexic children in the Castles and Coltheart study were all boys and aged between 8.5 and 14 years. Castles and Coltheart do not give details of the socio-economic status of the children, nor of their overall academic achievement level, but since they report that all were within the normal IQ range it is unlikely that the children were generally low achievers. The dyslexic children studied by Stanovich et al., in contrast, were 29 boys and 39 girls, all in third grade at school with mean age 8.9 years. They were from a district where "achievement levels in the schools tested are substantially below the norms of most standardized tests" (1997, p. 118). The sample of developmental dyslexics in the study carried out by Manis et al. comprised 14 girls and 37 boys, aged 9 to 15 years. Children were required to have a WISC IQ of at least 85 to be included in the study, and so the sample do not appear to differ in age or overall ability from the developmental dyslexics in the Castles and Coltheart study. However, different irregular word and nonword stimuli were used to test lexical and sub-lexical reading skill from those used by Castles and Coltheart (this also applies to the study of Stanovich et al., 1997). It will be important to ascertain whether sampling, task, and instructional differences can affect the outcome of sub-typing studies.

Stanovich et al., in discussing the results of their study, suggest that developmental surface dyslexia "may arise from a milder form of phonological deficit than that of the phonological dyslexic, but one conjoined with exceptionally inadequate reading experience" (1997, p. 123). In the studies reviewed in this chapter there is no evidence that the children and adults showing the pattern of developmental surface dyslexia had any less exposure to print or different reading instruction, compared to the dyslexics showing the pattern of phonological dyslexia. However, relevant details, such as the content of the reading curriculum and type and duration of remediation, have not been systematically recorded in the studies. A further argument against the interpretation of Stanovich et al. is that studies that have included measures of reading-related phonological skills (e.g., Hanley & Gard, 1995) have failed to demonstrate even mild levels of phonological deficit in clear-cut cases of developmental surface dyslexia. It would be necessary, as acknowledged by Stanovich et al., to carry out longitudinal studies in order to test their interpretation. Possible reasons for the lack of progress in uncovering the cause(s) of developmental surface dyslexia are discussed in the concluding section of this chapter.

REMEDIATION STUDIES WITH DEVELOPMENTAL SURFACE DYSLEXICS

Broom and Doctor (1995) have pointed out that while there are a number of remediation studies with acquired dyslexics based on a dual-route model of reading, there is a paucity of published model-based remedial studies with developmental dyslexics. Two such studies of developmental surface dyslexics are discussed next.

Seymour and Bunce (1994) carried out an assessment of the reading and spelling of two 8-year-old dyslexic boys. The assessment was based on Seymour's "dual foundation" model of reading development. According to this, orthographic, skilled reading is achieved through an interaction of: (1) alphabetic knowledge of letter–sound associations, (2) structures represented in a logographically stored vocabulary, and (3) an overall organisational framework contributed by phonological awareness skills. One of the dyslexic boys, RC, had a high error rate with irregular words and showed a tendency to make phonologically appropriate spelling errors. RC also showed a very marked length effect in terms of vocal reaction times, and equivalent dispersed reaction time patterns for words and nonwords. Seymour and Bunce concluded that RC did not seem to have efficient procedures for direct recognition of words or storage and production of specific spellings. They suggest that he had an impairment of the logographic process that resulted in a malformed orthographic framework.

Remediation for RC was aimed at constructing the orthographic framework. Establishment of the "core" structure (simple initial and terminal consonants and short vowels) was first emphasised. This was then expanded into a more complex form (consonant clusters and lengthened vowels). Lists of words embodying the orthographic framework structure were used in the intervention, which involved tasks such as anagram solving, rhyming, and alliteration. Following intervention RC showed a gain in performance but his reading continued to be affected by spelling–sound regularity and word length. Seymour and Bunce suggested that there was quantitative improvement without a change in reading strategy.

Broom and Doctor (1995) devised a remedial programme for an 11-year-old dyslexic boy, DF, whose pattern of performance on a range of tasks was indicative of surface dyslexia. Pre-therapy assessment involved a lexical decision task which was presented in both the visual and auditory modality. DF was significantly more accurate on the auditory than the visual version of the task, indicating that his poorer visual performance was not due to a general language problem, but to a specific reading difficulty. DF showed a significant regularity effect in reading regular and irregular words and his performance with the irregular words was significantly worse than that of 25 reading-age-matched control children; his performance with the regular words was better than that of the controls. 94% of DF's errors to irregular words were regularisations. When asked to define printed homophones, DF's definitions invariably corresponded with his pronunciation of the stimuli. Of 24 homophones read aloud correctly, 15 were defined as the wrong homophone (e.g. *write* was defined as "not the left"). 89% of spelling errors were phonologically appropriate.

Broom and Doctor found that DF's ability to read aloud irregular words was strongly affected by word frequency. They therefore suggested that lexical–orthographic representations had failed to be established for lower frequency words. A set of irregular words of varying frequency were chosen as materials for remediation. All were words that DF was able to define but was unable to read or spell correctly. Therapy involved a procedure adapted from Bradley (1981) and consisted of the repeated naming and spelling of the training words, as well as discussion of their meaning. There was a significant improvement in reading the treated items after the remediation but not in reading untreated irregular words. Performance on a homophone definition task did not change before and after remediation. Broom and Doctor conclude that the remediation had produced a quantitative change in DF's reading but had not resulted in a qualitative change in reading strategy. We saw previously that this was the same conclusion that was reached by Seymour and Bunce (1994) after remediation with RC. Broom and Doctor suggest however, that if reaction time had been included as a response measure (as in the studies of Seymour, 1986) it might have been possible to observe a change in processing strategy that was not observable from the simple accuracy measure that they employed.

CONCLUSIONS AND INDICATIONS FOR FUTURE RESEARCH

The studies reviewed in this chapter show that individuals with developmental dyslexia can differ in their reliance on lexical or sub-lexical procedures for reading and spelling. We saw that Coltheart et al. (1983) interpreted the difficulty in developmental surface dyslexia in terms of the dual route theory of reading, and suggested that the disorder involves a deficit within the lexical procedure. In a similar vein, Goulandris and Snowling (1991) suggest that surface dyslexia is due to inadequate or partial development of orthographic lexical representations. They also suggest that the problem can be interpreted in terms of Frith's (1985) stage model of the development of reading. This is the framework used by Hanley et al. (1992), who suggest that the disorder is the result of arrest at the alphabetic stage of development.

The range of possible interpretations of the deficit in developmental surface dyslexia indicates that there is room for improved knowledge of lexical–orthographic skills. There has been a vast amount of research into the precursors of sub-lexical reading skill in children, and also into the use of the sub-lexical procedure in children and skilled readers. However, there has been a dearth of research activity concerned with the development of the lexical procedure. We now need a detailed description of how normally developing readers acquire lexical representations. Investigative tools such as the format distortion and matching techniques used by Seymour (1986, 1987a, 1987b) and Hanley et al. (1992) could usefully be employed. It is only when we have a detailed understanding of the development of lexical–orthographic skill that we are likely to be able to understand why some developmental dyslexics fail to develop this process.

We also need to know more about the influence of variables such as instruction, remediation, and motivation (Stanovich et al., 1997; Wilding, 1989). With the exception of the study by Broom and Doctor (1995), which was specifically concerned with remediation, investigations of developmental surface dyslexia have rarely reported pertinent details. We have seen that there are cases where instruction or remediation are unlikely to have had a causative influence on the procedures being used for reading and spelling by developmental surface dyslexics. However, fine-grained information about the interaction of environmental and constitutional variables will be of both practical and theoretical use in furthering our understanding of the condition.

Finally, the issue of developmental surface dyslexia in languages other than English seems worthy of further investigation. There have only been two relevant studies, and both of these failed to report data from control participants, which means that their results cannot be considered conclusive. Further cross-language research and research on bilinguals is likely to be informative about the relationship between scripts and the lexical reading procedure.

REFERENCES

Backman, J., Bruck, M., Hebert, M., & Seidenberg, M.S. (1984). Acquisition and use of spelling-sound correspondences in reading. *Journal of Experimental Child Psychology, 38*, 114–133.

Beauvois, M.F., & Derousné, J. (1979). Phonological processes in reading: Data from alexia. *Journal of Neurology, Neurosurgery and Psychiatry, 42*, 1125–1132.

Boder, E. (1971). Developmental dyslexia: A diagnostic screening procedure based on three characteristic patterns of reading and spelling. In B. Bateman (Ed.), *Learning disorders*. Seattle, CA: Special Child Publications.

Boder, E. (1973). Developmental dyslexia: A diagnostic approach based on three atypical reading–spelling patterns. *Developmental Medicine and Child Neurology, 15*, 663–687.

Boder, E., & Jarrico, S. (1982). *The Boder test of reading–spelling patterns*. New York: Grune & Stratton.

Bradley, L. (1981). The organisation of motor patterns for spelling: An effective remedial strategy for backward readers. *Developmental Medicine and Child Neurology*, *23*, 83–91.

Broom, Y.M., & Doctor, E.A. (1995). Developmental surface dyslexia: A case study of the efficacy of a remediation programme. *Cognitive Neuropsychology, 12*, 69–110.

Bryant, P., & Impey, L. (1986). The similarities between normal readers and developmental and acquired dyslexics. *Cognition, 24*, 121–137.

Castles, A., & Coltheart, M. (1993). Varieties of developmental dyslexia. *Cognition, 47*, 149–180.

Coltheart, M. (1987). Varieties of developmental dyslexia: A comment on Bryant & Impey. *Cognition, 27*, 97–101.

Coltheart, M. (1981). Disorders of reading and their implications for models of normal reading. *Visible Language, 15*, 245–286.

Coltheart, M., Besner, D., Jonasson, J.T., & Davelaar, E. (1979). Phonological encoding in the lexical decision task. *Quarterly Journal of Experimental Psychology, 31*, 489–507.

Coltheart, M., Masterson, J., Byng, S., Prior, M., & Riddoch, J. (1983). Surface dyslexia. *Quarterly Journal of Experimental Psychology, 35A*, 469–495.

Denckla, M.B. (1977). Minimal brain dysfunction and dyslexia: Beyond diagnosis by exclusion. In M.E. Blaw, I. Rapin, & M. Kinsbourne (Eds), *Topics in child neurology*. New York: Spectrum.

Denckla, M.B. (1978). Minimal brain dysfunction. In J.S. Chall & A.F. Mirsky (Eds), *Education and the brain*. Chicago: University of Chicago Press.

Friedrich, F.J., Walker, J.A., & Posner, M.I. (1985). Effects of parietal lesions on visual matching: Implications for reading errors. *Cognitive Neuropsychology, 2*, 253–264.

Frith, U. (1985). Beneath the surface of developmental dyslexia. In K.E. Patterson, J.C. Marshall, & M. Coltheart (Eds), *Surface dyslexia: Neuropsychological and cognitive studies of phonological reading*. Hove, UK: Lawrence Erlbaum Associates Ltd.

Goulandris, N.K., & Snowling, M. (1991). Visual memory deficits: A plausible cause of developmental dyslexia? Evidence from a single case study. *Cognitive Neuropsychology, 8*, 127–154.

Hanley, J.R. (1997). Reading and spelling impairments in undergraduate students with developmental dyslexia. *Journal of Research in Reading, 20*, 22–30.

Hanley, J.R., & Gard, F. (1995). A dissociation between developmental surface and phonological dyslexia in two undergraduate students. *Neuropsychologia, 33*, 909–914.

Hanley, J.R., Hastie, K., & Kay, J. (1992). Developmental surface dyslexia and dysgraphia: An orthographic processing impairment. *Quarterly Journal of Experimental Psychology, 44*, 285–319.

Holmes, J.M. (1973). *Dyslexia: A neurolinguistic study of traumatic and developmental disorders of reading*. Unpublished PhD thesis, University of Edinburgh, UK.

Holmes, J.M. (1978). "Regression" and reading breakdown. In A. Caramazza & E.B. Zurif (Eds.), *Language acquisition and language breakdown: Parallels and divergences* (pp. 87–98). Baltimore, MD: Johns Hopkins Press.

Job, R., Sartori, G., Masterson, J., & Coltheart, M. (1984). Developmental surface dyslexia in Italian. In R.N. Malatesha & H.A. Whitaker (Eds), *Dyslexia: A global issue* (pp. 133–141). The Hague, The Netherlands: Martinus Nijhoff.

Kay, J., Lesser, R., & Coltheart, M. (1992). *Psycholinguistic assessment of language processing in aphasia* [PALPA]. Hove, UK: Lawrence Erlbaum Associates Ltd.

Kinsbourne, M., & Warrington, E.K. (1963). Developmental factors in reading and writing backwardness. *British Journal of Psychology, 54*, 145–156.

Lepschy, A.L., & Lepschy, G. (1981). *La lingua Italiana*. Milan, Italy: Bompiani.

Manis, F.R., Seidenberg, M.S., Doi, L.M., McBride-Chang, C., & Petersen, A. (1996). On the bases of two subtypes of developmental dyslexia. *Cognition, 58*, 157–195.

Marcel, A.J. (1980). Surface dyslexia and beginning reading: A revised hypothesis of the pronunciation of print and its impairments. In M. Coltheart, K.E. Patterson, & J.C. Marshall (Eds), *Deep dyslexia* (pp. 227–258). London: Routledge & Kegan Paul.

Marshall, J.C., & Newcombe, F. (1973). Patterns of paralexia: A psycholinguistic approach. *Journal of Psycholinguistic Research, 2,* 175–199.

Masterson, J. (1983). *Surface dyslexia and the operation of the phonological route in reading.* Unpublished PhD thesis, University of London, UK.

Masterson, J. (1984). Surface dyslexia and its relationship to developmental disorders of reading. *Visible Language, 18,* 388–396.

Masterson, J., Coltheart, M., & Meara, P. (1985). Surface dyslexia in a language without irregularly spelled words. In K.E. Patterson, J.C. Marshall, & M. Coltheart (Eds), *Surface dyslexia: Neuropsychological and cognitive studies of phonological reading* (pp. 215–224). Hove, UK: Lawrence Erlbaum Associates Ltd.

Masterson, J., Laxon, V., & Stuart, M. (1992). Beginning reading with phonology. *British Journal of Psychology, 83,* 1–12.

Mattis, S., French, J.S., & Rapin, I. (1975). Dyslexia in children and young adults: Three independent neuropsychological syndromes. *Developmental Medicine and Child Neurology, 17,* 150–163.

Morton, J., & Patterson, K.E. (1980). A new attempt at an interpretation, or, an attempt at a new interpretation. In M. Coltheart, K.E. Patterson, & J.C. Marshall (Eds), *Deep dyslexia* (pp. 91–118). London: Routledge & Kegan Paul.

Seymour, P.H.K. (1986). *Cognitive analysis of dyslexia.* London: Routledge & Kegan Paul.

Seymour, P.H.K. (1987a). Individual cognitive analysis of competent and impaired reading. *British Journal of Psychology, 78,* 483–506.

Seymour, P.H.K. (1987b). Word recognition processes: An analysis based on format distortion effects. In J.R. Beech & A.M. Colley (Eds), *Cognitive approaches to reading.* Chichester, UK: John Wiley.

Seymour, P.H.K., & Bunce, F. (1994). Application of cognitive models to remediation in cases of developmental dyslexia. In M.J. Riddoch & G.W. Humphreys (Eds), *Cognitive neuropsychology and cognitive rehabilitation* (pp. 349–378). Hove, UK: Lawrence Erlbaum Associates Ltd.

Seymour, P.H.K., & Evans, H.M. (1993). The visual (orthographic) processor and developmental dyslexia. In D.M. Willows, R.S. Kruk, & E. Corcos (Eds), *Visual processes in reading and reading disabilities* (pp. 347–376). Hove, UK: Lawrence Erlbaum Associates Ltd.

Shallice, T. (1981). Neurological impairment of cognitive processes. *British Medical Bulletin, 37,* 187–192.

Shallice, T., & Warrington, E.K. (1980). Single and multiple component central dyslexic syndromes. In M. Coltheart, K.E. Patterson, & J.C. Marshall (Eds), *Deep dyslexia* (pp. 119–145). London: Routledge & Kegan Paul.

Smith, M.M. (1970). *Patterns of intellectual abilities in educationally handicapped children.* Unpublished PhD thesis, Claremont College, CA.

Snowling, M.J. (1983). The comparison of acquired and developmental disorders of reading— A discussion. *Cognition, 14,* 105–118.

Snowling, M., & Hulme, C. (1989). A longitudinal case of developmental phonological dyslexia. *Cognitive Neuropsychology, 6,* 379–401.

Stanovich, K.E., Siegel, L.S., & Gottardo, A. (1997). Converging evidence for phonological and surface subtypes of reading disability. *Journal of Educational Psychology, 89,* 114–127.

Temple, C.M. (1984). New approaches to the developmental dyslexias. In F.C. Rose (Ed.), *Advances in neurology: Vol. 42: Progress in aphasiology* (pp. 223–232). New York: Raven Press.

Temple, C.M. (1985). Surface dyslexia: Variations within a syndrome. In K.E. Patterson, J.C.

Marshall & M. Coltheart (Eds), *Surface dyslexia: Neuropsychological and cognitive studies of phonological reading* (pp 269–288). Hove, UK: Lawrence Erlbaum Associates Ltd.

Temple, C.M. (1987). The nature of normality, the deviance of dyslexia and the recognition of rhyme: A reply to Bryant & Impey (1986). *Cognition, 27,* 103–108.

Temple, C.M., & Marshall, J. (1983). A case study of developmental phonological dyslexia. *British Journal of Psychology, 74,* 517–533.

Waters, G.S., Seidenberg, M.S., & Bruck, M. (1984). Children's and adults' use of spelling–sound information in three reading tasks. *Memory and Cognition, 12,* 293–305.

Wilding, J. (1989). Developmental dyslexics do not fit in boxes: Evidence from the case studies. *European Journal of Cognitive Psychology, 1,* 105–127.

Wilding, J. (1990). Developmental dyslexics do not fit in boxes: Evidence from six new case studies. *European Journal of Cognitive Psychology, 2,* 97–131.

Author Index

149

Subject Index